GREEK AND ROMAN
PORTRAITS

SUSAN WALKER

GREEK AND ROMAN PORTRAITS

Published for the Trustees of the British Museum
by British Museum Press

To the memory of my parents, Edith and Bill Cook, who took
great interest in people, dress and the art of portraiture

© 1995 The Trustees of the British Museum

Published by British Museum Press
A division of British Museum Publications Ltd
46 Bloomsbury Street, London WC1B 3QQ

British Library Cataloguing in Publication Data
A catalogue record for this book is available from the British Library

ISBN 0–7141–2203–3

Designed by Andrew Shoolbred
Cover designed by Grahame Dudley Associates

Photoset in Garamond No. 3 by
Rowland Phototypesetting Ltd, Bury St Edmunds, Suffolk
Printed in Great Britain by
The Bath Press Ltd, Avon

Frontispiece: Marble head of the 'Pseudo-Seneca' (see fig. 30, p.49).

Front Cover: Marble bust of a bearded man in oratorical dress; said to be from
Athens and made about AD 150. This portrait reflects contemporary interest in
classical Greek culture, of which its unnamed subject was apparently a
distinguished exponent.

Contents

	Preface and Acknowledgements	6
1	Introduction	7
2	What is a Portrait For?	16
3	The Beginnings of Greek Portraiture	28
4	Portraits of Greeks in the Roman World	41
5	Greek Portraits of Rulers	50
6	The Imperial Image of Augustus	61
7	The Roman Image	72
8	Bearded and Beardless Men	83
9	Dress	94
10	Epilogue	108
	Further Reading	110
	Illustration Credits	110
	Index	111

Preface and Acknowledgements

This short book arises from a course of eight lectures on Greek and Roman portraits given to undergraduates at Cambridge University in 1992. I realised then that, while there existed some indispensable compendia of Greek and Hellenistic portraits and a first-rate study of Augustus' use of imagery, there was no brief introduction to Greek and Roman portraiture in print in the English language.

Many will remember with pleasure the late Roger Hinks' work *Greek and Roman Portrait Sculpture*, first printed by the British Museum in 1935 and reissued by British Museum Publications in 1976. I cannot emulate Hinks' sensitivity to the spiritual element in ancient portraiture, but here offer what I hope will be stimulating observations on a genre of considerable interest and relevance to modern life.

I am most grateful to Lucilla Burn, Hero Granger-Taylor, John Wilkes, Dyfri Williams and Susan Woodford, who read early drafts of all or part of the text. Numerous improvements were suggested by Anne Marriott. I am also grateful to Nina Shandloff, Colin Grant and Teresa Francis for their help and encouragement. All remaining errors are of course my own responsibility. Spellings of Greek names are a problem in a book of this sort. Place names and names of famous Greeks are Latinised where this is the familiar form to the modern reader; the names of sculptors and vase-painters appear in Hellenised form. The chapter on 'Bearded and beardless men', is slightly modified from my article 'Bearded men' which first appeared in the *Journal of the History of Collections* 3, no. 2 (1991), 265–77, and I thank Arthur Macgregor for permission to reproduce it here. The photographs of British Museum objects were produced with customary speed by Nic Nicholls, with help from Ken Evans and Lloyd Gallimore, and the drawings are by Susan Bird. A full list of illustration acknowledgements appears on page 110.

CHAPTER 1

Introduction

This book is concerned with portraits of living or recently deceased persons in Greek and Roman antiquity, and also with images of individuals – some historical, some perhaps mythical – created long after their supposed lifetimes. They include metal or stone statues, life-sized or larger; busts and statuettes of metal, stone and terracotta; painted portraits, images worked into mosaic pavements, and portraits engraved on gems and coins. The timespan covers more than a millennium, from about 700 BC to AD 400, a period in which the Greek and Roman world experienced profound political, social and economic change.

In the seventh century BC the Greeks lived in independent territories, in which arose the city-states such as Athens, Corinth, Argos and Sparta that were to dominate archaic and classical Greece from the sixth to the fourth centuries BC. Though the Greek city-states enjoyed independent political constitutions, and often fought with each other over territory or issues of local or wider mastery, some aspects of archaic and classical society encouraged a more coherent vision of Greek identity, reflected in the art of the period. There were, for example, religious sanctuaries, such as those of the gods Apollo and Zeus at Delphi and Olympia respectively, at which all Greeks worshipped. Early in their history, these sanctuaries became showcases for images not only of rulers, whether local or more distant, but also of rich and influential private patrons.

Relationships with external powers also influenced the development of portraiture in the Greek world. Persian kings controlled Greek cities in western Asia Minor for extended periods in the sixth and fourth centuries BC, and invaded mainland Greece itself in the fifth. When faced with such an external threat, most of the Greek city-states formed alliances, but the repulse of the Persians effectively strengthened those individual cities, notably Athens and Sparta, whose citizens had led the fight to retain independence.

Within these and other Greek communities distinctive political systems evolved. Thus, while Sparta was governed from archaic to Hellenistic times by two kings and a council of elders, Athens was in the later sixth century ruled by a dynasty of tyrants, who were overthrown in 510 BC in favour of a democratic regime. In the fifth century the wars against the Persians saw the rise of a number of powerful politician-generals, of whom Pericles of Athens had perhaps the most significant influence upon the portrayal of individuals, both in his own day and many centuries after his death. The brilliant culture of many classical Greek cities, especially Athens, encouraged the rise of extraordinary individuals, in particular playwrights such as Sophocles and Euripides, and the philosophers Socrates and Plato, whose portraits were later avidly collected by Roman admirers.

The fifth century ended as it had begun, with war; this time between the empire of Athens, where individual political responsibility was

1 *Marble herm of the Athenian statesman and general Pericles (about 500–429 BC), inscribed in Greek with his name; Roman version found at Tivoli, near Rome, of an original made in Pericles' lifetime about 450 BC and now lost. The writer Plutarch noted that Pericles was almost always portrayed in a helmet to conceal his squill-shaped head.*

2 Marble statuette of Socrates, the founder of Attic philosophy (469–399 BC); from Alexandria, where it was probably made in the second century BC. The artist has captured Socrates' penetrating gaze, for which he was famous. However, this statuette is likely to be an independent Hellenistic creation differing from other surviving versions of an official portrait devised after Socrates' death.

emphasised, and the allies of Sparta, where individual interest was sacrificed to foster a collective military discipline. Though the Spartans emerged victorious, their military leaders proved ineffective peacetime governors, and in the course of the fourth century BC the independent city-states of old Greece withered while major new powers grew on the fringes of the Greek world.

These kingdoms proved most important in the development of portraiture. In south-west Asia Minor, the kings of Lycia were the first to put their portraits on coinage used to pay mercenary armies. The dynast Mausolus, ruler of neighbouring Caria, and a dominant figure in the region, was commemorated after his death in 353 BC in a grand monument with three-dimensional sculptured portraits and other figures representing life at his court. Within Greece, conflict was caused by the rise of the Macedonian rulers to the north. Individuals engaged in the struggle are known even today from their portraits, notably the Athenian politicians Demosthenes, who opposed Macedonian control, and Aeschines, who was said to have betrayed Athens to the Macedonians.

3 Below left *Marble head of the Athenian orator Demosthenes (c. 384–322 BC), restored as a herm. Like his other portraits, of which some fifty survive, this is a Roman version of a lost Greek bronze original by Polyeuktos of Athens, commissioned in 280 BC.*

4 Below right *Inscribed marble portrait herm of the orator Aeschines of Athens (c. 390/389 – after 314 BC); Roman version found at Bitolia in Macedonia. A draped statue of Aeschines from Herculaneum suggests a date for the lost Greek original of c. 325–300 BC, when Macedon, whose cause was supported by Aeschines, controlled Greece.*

Within three decades of the death of Mausolus, the Macedonians had
conquered Greece and the territories of the Persian Empire by military
force accompanied by a cultural programme which portrayed the victors
as liberators – in the style of the fifth-century Greek opponents of Persian
rule. However, the Macedonian Empire did not survive intact the death
in 323 BC of its charismatic ruler Alexander the Great; lands won by
Alexander were divided amongst his generals, whose descendants
formed dynasties ruling the reduced territories known to modern
scholars as the Hellenistic kingdoms. Alexander, who was not yet thirty-
three when he died, had considerable influence over Hellenistic ruler-
portraiture and even over the development of Roman ruler portraits
when the Roman Republic collapsed in the first century BC.

By that time most of the Hellenistic kingdoms had fallen to the
Romans, who had emerged as the most powerful community in the
Mediterranean following their defeat of Carthage in the third century

*5 Detail of a mosaic
pavement showing Alexander
the Great of Macedon
fighting the Persian king
Darius at the Battle of the
Issus in 334 BC.
Alexander's head is bare to
allow recognition of the
principal protagonist in a
crowded battle scene. The
pavement was made for a
villa at Pompeii in the first
century BC and was probably
based on an earlier painting,
now lost.*

6 *Marble head of the Roman general Gnaeus Pompeius Magnus (Pompey: 106–48 BC). Pompey has copied the hairstyle of the Macedonian ruler Alexander the Great (see fig. 5), but this is combined with carefully observed Roman facial features, such as the small eyes, narrow lips and bulbous nose. This portrait was found in Rome in the tomb of the Licinii family and may date from the time of Marcus Licinius Crassus Frugi, consul in AD 27, who gave his son the name of Gnaeus Pompeius Magnus to mark his descent from Pompey through his mother.*

BC. Rome's most striking characteristic, one not shared by classical Greek city-states, was her openness to external influence, a trait visible from the earliest record of Rome as a city, when she was governed by Etruscan kings. According to tradition, the kings were expelled and a republican constitution formulated at about the time the tyrants were overthrown in Athens in the late sixth century BC. The Republic was governed by elected magistrates, of whom the most senior were two consuls, a power-sharing arrangement reminiscent of the Spartan double kingship. No securely dated portraits survive from the early years of the Republic, though later literary sources and archaeological evidence indicate a long-standing interest in ancestral portraiture. Portraiture was, however, to make a great impact in public life at Rome when the Republic became seriously weakened in the first century BC. Rome was by then an imperial power, controlling all of Italy and many overseas territories. In the eastern Mediterranean, Roman generals were hailed as successors to the Hellenistic kings, and the images of some individuals, notably Gnaeus Pompeius Magnus (Pompey), who like Alexander was styled 'the Great', were strongly influenced by Hellenistic royal portraits.

Indeed, at Rome in the first century BC portraiture became a political medium, with rival military leaders using images of their noble ancestors or of themselves to advertise their fitness to rule and to proclaim their authority over the armies they controlled. Of particular importance

6

for his unprecedented regal use of portraiture was Julius Caesar, *dictator* at Rome from 48 BC until his assassination in 44 BC. His great-nephew and heir Octavian, who later became Augustus, the first emperor of Rome, was especially concerned with his image. He rejected the republican type of portrait abused by Caesar and, after formally proclaiming the restoration of the Republic in 27 BC, adopted instead an image derived from the ideal portrayal of the human figure developed in classical Greece.

In imperial Rome, portraits of emperors and their families, now widely recognised from images on coins and from statues set up in public places, had enormous impact upon the form of portraits of private individuals. In various parts of the Roman Empire, commemorative funerary portraits were made for the first time. Surviving examples reveal an interest in copying court hairstyles, contemporary jewellery and dress, even imperial features. Emperors developed a distinctive family likeness which lasted until the collapse of their dynasty. After the suicide in AD 68 of Nero, the last of the Julio-Claudian emperors to succeed Augustus, there ensued eighteen months of civil war. The emergent emperor, Titus Flavius Vespasianus (Vespasian), was of relatively modest origin, a fact made clear in his homely portraits which, in

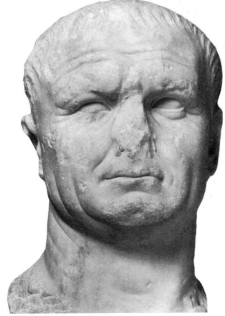

7 *Marble head from a statue of Vespasian (emperor AD 69–79). Found at Carthage in north Africa, this portrait well captures the military bearing of Vespasian, who came to power as eventual victor in a civil war that produced four emperors in a year. The form of the portrait recalls that of Roman republican figures such as Pompey (fig. 6) and reflects the emperor's relatively modest social origins.*

marked contrast to the sophisticated images of the youthful Nero, recall those of private citizens in late republican Rome. Vespasian's features were reflected in private portraiture under the Flavian dynasty, which ended with the murder of his younger son Domitian in AD 96.

Even when an emperor succeeded by adoption, as most second-century emperors did, some continuity of image is evident. Though Hadrian, who succeeded as Trajan's adopted heir in AD 117, broke with tradition by being the first Roman emperor to wear a beard, his adopted successor Antoninus Pius (AD 138–61) wore his hair in similar fashion to suggest a physical resemblance to his predecessor. When the Antonine dynasty ended, after the murder of Commodus in 192, a civil war followed. The victorious Lucius Septimius Severus, of North African origin, adopted the Antonine name for his elder son and devised a portrait suggesting political and cultural continuity. However, when the military revolted against Alexander Severus in AD 235 to end the Severan dynasty, central imperial authority collapsed and the Empire was ruled by a succession of soldier-emperors. Their portraits reflect their provincial origin and rough route to power; only the emperor Gallienus (AD 253–67) reveals in his portraits an educated and refined metropolitan Roman background.

8

8 *Coin (left) of the emperor Maximinus Thrax (AD 235–238), with close-cropped hair and beard, and medallion (right) of the emperor Gallienus (AD 253–268), whose long hair and naked shoulders recall the style of the philhellene emperors Nero and Hadrian.*

Central authority was finally restored by Diocletian in AD 284, fifty years after the fall of the Severans. Diocletian introduced a collegiate system of government, with two senior emperors (*augusti*) and two junior colleagues (*caesares*); the two pairs (each consisting of a senior and a junior colleague) were responsible for administering the western and eastern provinces respectively. The collective nature of Diocletian's tetrarchy was reflected in imperial portraiture, in which it is difficult to identify the features of individual members of the college of emperors.

While effective in restoring imperial authority, Diocletian's reforms did not long outlast him. The emperor Constantine (AD 306–37) developed a portrait deliberately recalling (but in a contemporary idiom) the images of Augustus.

Most peoples living in the Roman provinces of the eastern Mediterranean continued to speak Greek as their common language, and many aspects of classical Greek culture survived not only the imposition of Roman rule but also the adoption of Christianity as the official religion of the Empire. Schools of Greek philosophy survived in Athens and elsewhere until an edict of closure by the emperor Justinian in AD 529. Some of the most vivid portraits of famous individuals of pagan classical Greece were made in late antiquity, and were even used in the decoration of, for example, mosaic pavements. Greek dress was worn by many throughout antiquity, changing remarkably little between classical times and the late Empire. These aspects of cultural continuity are emphasised in this book which, though not ignoring cultural and regional influences upon portraiture, draws attention to the close relationship between Greek and Roman ideas about the commemoration of the individual in a portrait.

CHAPTER 2

What is a Portrait For?

It was decreed by the Senate that a golden image of Faustina be carried on a chair into the theatre whenever the emperor was to be a spectator, and that the effigy be placed in the box where the living Faustina had always sat; around it were to sit the women of the foremost families of Rome (Dio Cassius, 72, 31, 1).

The manner in which the gilded portrait of the late empress – who died in AD 141, early in the reign of her husband Antoninus Pius (AD 138–61) – was addressed in their conversations is left to the imagination. The anecdote of Faustina's effigy offers a fine example of one of the principal functions of portraiture: to defy death by preserving a likeness of the deceased. It also illustrates the Roman taste for using portraits to act the part of the dead or, in some instances, of individuals alive but personally inaccessible: statues of emperors, for example, were sometimes petitioned for justice or asylum, as if they were living beings.

Neither Latin nor ancient Greek had a precise equivalent for the modern term 'portrait', which appears in several languages in approximately similar form, and is ultimately derived from the Latin *protrahere*, to drag out. As we understand it, a portrait is a record of the appearance and character of an individual singled out from the crowd. In antiquity, *protrahere* was used in a more literal sense for much less agreeable activities, such as dragging a person by the hair or eviscerating a slaughtered animal. The closest ancient equivalents to the modern term, the Greek word *eikon*, used by Dio Cassius to describe the portrait of Faustina in the passage quoted above, and the Latin *imago*, are better translated as 'image', a term linked to a mental process much used in the interpretation of portraiture, imagination.

We use our imagination to answer for ourselves the questions posed by ancient and modern portraits. Has the artist succeeded in conveying the character of the person represented? Are his or her physical character-

9 *Marble relief, Roman, about* AD
*160–80, commemorating a soldier who
died at the age of twenty-nine and was
named Ares, after the Greek god of war.
A figure (left), perhaps Ares, appears in
military dress, his right hand holding an
offering above a flaming altar, his left a
scroll. Another figure (right) stands in
civilian dress, with helmet and weapons
beside him, perhaps a reference to the text
below, which describes Ares leaving his
weapons to journey into the other world
where nothing exists but darkness.*

istics faithfully reproduced? Are we given a sense of the social origin of
the subject? Was the portrait made to mark a particular achievement, or
the passing of a stage in life, such as formal entry into adulthood, the
contract of marriage, the birth of a child, or death? We expect much of
modern portraits, asking such questions of images of persons known and
unknown, sometimes rejecting an image of a familiar individual as 'not a
true likeness', and demanding as high a standard of an amateur
photographer as of a distinguished artist. What then are we to expect of
ancient portraits?

Some do indeed convey character, and many more a sense of individuality. The convincing depiction of character may represent a victory for
the artist, in the sense of gaining some control from the patron over the
form of the portrait, though examples abound both from antiquity and
from more recent times of attempts by prominent public figures to
influence the representation of his or her character. Alexander the Great
of Macedon (336–323 BC) is said to have controlled the form of his
portrait by personally appointing the artists he considered most gifted at

depicting his character. One would give much for a contemporary account of how many artists were discarded before the first Roman emperor Augustus (27 BC–AD 14) approved the blandly classicising form of his official portraits.

To the modern viewer, accuracy in recording physical features may seem the most pressing demand of a portrait, but true representation can hardly be confirmed in ancient portraiture. Moreover, even photography can be deceptive in this respect: most celebrities turn out to be shorter in real life than in their pictures, and the film star Marilyn Monroe was surely exceptional in appearing in her photographs ten pounds lighter than her true weight.

That austere Roman, Cato the Elder, is said to have mocked enthusiasts of portraiture, though even he eventually succumbed to the honour of a public statue. He claimed that, in making so much of the works of bronze-smiths and painters, those who favoured the granting of public statues overlooked Cato's own achievement as Censor: by his moral guidance, wise restraint and teachings, the citizens of Rome carried the best portraits of themselves in their souls (Plutarch, *Life of the Elder Cato*, 19). So they did, but it is the drawing out of that portrait in the soul that proves the skill of the artist. The artist's success in conveying the character of the subject is easier to evaluate, especially at a distance of thousands of years, than the accuracy of his rendering of flesh.

More accessible than character to the modern viewer of ancient portraits is any sign of the social origin of the subject. Amongst the clues provided by the artist, the most helpful are inscriptions naming the subject, of which many survive from antiquity, often carefully placed in association with the individual image. Artists were equally adept at showing social origins visually, in dress, in pose, or by indicating the setting in a relief sculpture or painting. Dress may reflect not only social rank but a specific role in public or private life, such as priestess, magistrate or courtesan. Pose is also telling: a seated figure was, throughout antiquity, an individual of authority or elevated status, whether a god (all mortals on the Parthenon frieze stand if they are not on horseback, whereas the gods are seated), a ruler, or the master or mistress of a Greek household.

Dress, pose and setting may also offer answers to the question of whether a portrait marks a particular stage in life. Marriage and death

10 Opposite *Marble relief commemorating Glykilla; said to have been found at Thebes in Boeotia and made about 410–400 BC. She sits on a chair, with her feet resting on a stool, while a standing maid offers jewellery from a* pyxis *(jewellery box).*

10

were the stages most frequently commemorated in ancient portraiture. The act of commemoration, the celebration of public honours and the display of personal wealth or social status provided occasions for the commissioning of portraits and remain so even today.

Far from drawing a person out from the crowd, a portrait may rather confirm the subject's membership of a group. In such portraits, the group itself is exclusive. Roman group portraits on privately commissioned monuments most often represent families of freedmen and women, former slaves who celebrated their right to legitimate marriage on acquiring their freedom. Portraits of freedmen also mark their subjects' transitional status as former aliens whose children had the right to Roman citizenship. It was therefore important to freedmen to portray the family as a newly legitimised group, and one of Roman appearance, despite the telling evidence of the alien names below the portraits.

Families of aristocrats are a recurring subject, notably in oil paintings of the Renaissance and later ages. In antiquity, aristocratic groups were certainly commissioned as early as the sixth century BC, but at that date portraits did not normally reproduce the personal characteristics of their subjects; individuals were identified by inscribed names. Most ancient aristocratic group portraits were not painted or carved in relief but were carved or cast, if metal, in the round. Such groups of free-standing figures usually survive only in part, and it is impossible to reconstruct the order in which they were originally placed unless we have inscriptions or literary references which make it clear. It is, however, evident from surviving monuments that free-standing portraits were placed in significant arrangements reflecting social relationships in real life. In the monumental tomb commissioned for Mausolus, ruler of Caria (south-west Asia Minor) in the mid-fourth century BC, over-life-sized portrait statues of the members of his court were set between the columns on the top of the tomb's podium. If we knew the identities of these portraits, we would know by name the most important people at Mausolus' court.

Five centuries later, about AD 150, a grandiose fountain was built by the Athenian millionaire Herodes Atticus in the sanctuary of Zeus at Olympia in Greece. The basin wall contained two storeys of statues, in which members of Herodes' family were displayed in an horizontal order reflecting their family relationships and in a vertical order suggesting a

11 Opposite *Reconstructed drawing of the Mausoleum at Halicarnassus, completed about 350 BC. The drawing shows how the sculpture may have been arranged on the building, with the figures standing in order between the columns and sculptures of various scales set on the podium below to represent scenes of battle and life at Mausolus' court.*

1, V

12

12 *Reconstructed drawing of the nymphaeum of Herodes Atticus at Olympia, Greece, built about AD 150. In the upper storey are statues of members of Herodes' family (left to right): his daughter Elpinice; Marcus Appius Bradua, grandfather of Herodes' wife Regilla; Atilia Caucidia Tertulla, mother of Regilla; Appius Annius Gallus, father of Regilla; Regilla; Zeus, the god who presided over the waters captured for the aqueduct feeding the nymphaeum; Herodes; Tiberius Claudius Atticus, father of Herodes; Vibullia Alcia, mother of*

comparison with members of the Roman imperial family. As the composition of the families changed by marriage or death, and children grew to adulthood, the statues were updated. As a group portrait, the gallery of Herodes' family at Olympia has hardly been surpassed.

We may expect to gain little notion of, say, Mausolus' or Herodes' actual appearance from the portraits on these monuments, for they reflect a tendency, especially pronounced in the Greek world, to heroise or idealise the personal characteristics of an individual honoured with a public statue. It was important, though, for the illiterate to be able to recognise the subject of a ruler portrait, such as Mausolus, and in other surviving portraits Herodes himself was well characterised as an ascetic philosopher, an image somewhat at odds with surviving accounts of his life. Ancient portraits of women were, with some significant exceptions, less naturalistic than those of men, a characteristic that may be observed

both in the portraits of women on the Mausoleum at Halicarnassus and in the much later portraits of women from Herodes' fountain at Olympia.

The elder Pliny, writing in the first century AD, observes (*Natural History*, XXXV, 9):

> Nor must we pass over a rather new invention, that of setting up portraits in libraries, if not of gold or silver at least of bronze, of those immortal spirits who speak to us in these places; in fact, even portraits of those whose looks were never modelled are made, and our sense of longing gives birth to faces which have not been recorded, as happens to be the case with Homer.

The fashion for retrospective portraiture began as soon as recognisable portraits were made in the fifth century BC. Thus the fifth-century image

12 (cont.) *Herodes; Atticus Bradua, son of Herodes; Athenais and Regillus, daughter and son of Herodes. In the lower register are portraits of members of the imperial family (left to right): Titus Aelius Antoninus and Annia Faustina; Domitia Faustina; the future emperor Lucius Verus; Faustina the Elder, empress of (right) the reigning emperor Antoninus Pius; Zeus; the deified emperor Hadrian; Hadrian's empress Sabina; the future emperor Marcus Aurelius; his future empress the younger Faustina; Lucilla, future empress of Lucius Verus.*

13 Above *Portrait of the blind poet Homer; Roman marble version of a lost classical Greek original created about 460 BC, some three centuries after Homer's supposed lifetime.*

14 Above right *Portrait of Homer; Roman marble herm, a version of a lost Hellenistic Greek original created about 100 BC; found in 1780 at Baia on the Bay of Naples. This image of Homer clearly indicates advanced age, and misleadingly suggests that the artist was familiar with the poet's personal appearance. It is likely that the artist was influenced by contemporary interest in the realistic recording of personal features.*

of the blind poet Homer, who had lived – if we may credit his existence at all – in the eighth century BC, is easily distinguishable from the second-century portrait of the same individual, though both types are preserved only in the form of marble versions made centuries later for Roman connoisseurs.

Portraits invented long after their subjects had died may hardly be expected to fulfil the function of defying death: Homer lived on, but only in the rarified climate of the gentleman's library. In contrast, some portraits commissioned for contemporaries, especially for the young who died before their time, often have a strong impact on the modern viewer, because the artist has succeeded in conveying not only individual character, but also a distinctive appearance that gives a sense of place. Painted portraits are particularly compelling in this respect: many of the painted panel portraits of Roman Egypt reproduce a physical type still current in north-east Africa, lean and spare, with large dark eyes and curly hair. As in so many Roman portraits, the eyes are used to draw in the viewer, who may begin to feel a personal acquaintance with the subject. Even though she has lost her nose, a woman from Carthage,

13

14

77

VII

II

portrayed in marble at the turn of the first and second centuries AD, seems real enough, perhaps because her extraordinarily elaborate coiffure is combined with all-too-human unplucked and straggling eyebrows and a homely round face.

Through the ages portraits have been created to address specific individuals or groups, and many images have been deliberately intended for an audience not personally acquainted with the subject. There are often substantial differences between images made for intimates and those intended to be viewed by unknown audiences. Today the difference lies between informality amongst intimates and the controlled formality of an official portrait, a distinction popularised by the invention of photography. In antiquity, the distinction lay between modesty in coins or statues made for public circulation and extravagance among intimates at court, the latter well expressed in the Hellenistic Greek and Roman cameo portraits made, like the painted miniatures of Elizabethan England, for courtiers and loyal officials.

Like imperial statues, ancient funerary portraits addressed the unknown viewer, and were often accompanied by inscriptions appealing to the attention of the casual passer-by not bound to the dead by social obligation. Greek and Roman funerary monuments were set up beside roads just outside the boundaries of cities, in sites deliberately intended to attract the attention of travellers and well suited to the display of personal accomplishment and social status. The latter could be indicated generally by the opulence of the monument or more specifically by dress or pose, or even by relative size – the small figures on classical Greek and later funerary reliefs are more often servants than children. Competitive display of personal wealth was recurrent in antiquity, and funerary monuments were occasionally the subject of restrictive legislation aimed at reducing social division. Dress, too, was sometimes the subject of such sumptuary laws, indicating the importance of clothing as an expression of personal wealth and social status.

Objects, clothing or scenery were sometimes used to refer specifically to the subject's personal distinction. An instructive late antique example is offered by the lid of the sarcophagus of Proclus, probably a native of Aix-en-Provence in southern France, who had successfully competed in oratorical contests held in Italy. The accompanying text, written in elegant Homeric hexameters, has his widow Rufina describing a fine

15 Above *Part of the marble sarcophagus of the orator Proclus, shown (left) as the victor in the contests mentioned in the accompanying Greek verse inscription. Said to be from Aix-en-Provence and made about AD 300.*

16 Opposite *Inscribed marble portrait of the lyric poet Pindar (c. 518 – after 446 BC), found with many other portraits of famous Greeks in a late Roman philosophical school at Aphrodisias in Caria. One of a series of portraits set in roundels to decorate the walls of the school courtyard.*

tomb with gleaming doors and a statue of the late orator exactly resembling him. In the relief beside the inscription, Proclus appears leaning on a column in oratorical dress, displaying a branch of laurel to mark his success.

Few portraits, however, are as simple as they seem, and the symbols used by the artist require careful study to reach an understanding of ancient representations of individuals. The modern viewer must guard against preconceived ideas and expectations of how certain individuals should appear. Scholarship received a rude shock with the recent discovery at Aphrodisias in Asia Minor of an inscribed late Roman portrait of the Greek lyric poet Pindar. The face was familiar from other surviving portraits, but without the evidence of a contemporary inscription had until then been taken to represent the austere soldier-king Pausanias of Sparta.

CHAPTER 3

The Beginnings of Greek Portraiture

A rchaic and classical Greek representations of individuals rarely reproduced the personal features of the subject, but illustrated his or her moral qualities, specific achievements or position in life and, in some instances, ethnic origin. Individual identity was recorded in an accompanying inscription, which in an archaic statue might appear on the figure itself but in a classical work was more likely to be inscribed on the base on which the figure was set.

A greater number of identified figures has survived from the sixth century BC, when much high-quality work was executed in marble, than from the fifth, when the preferred medium was bronze, now mostly lost. Thus a portrait of Chares, ruler of Teichioussa in south-west Asia Minor in the sixth century BC, may be identified by the name and title written on his throne, but the identity of the fifth-century discus-thrower (*Discobolus*), a famous work by the sculptor Myron, remains unknown to us, as the original bronze with its accompanying inscribed base is lost. The figure survives only in marble versions made for Roman connoisseurs, with no identifying text. The original Discobolus was commissioned to celebrate an athletic victory, and the name of the victorious individual would have been inscribed on the base on which the sculpture was set. Though honouring only one individual, the composition worked rather like a modern war memorial, where the idealised figure of an unknown soldier is sculpted on the top, and on the base appears a list of the individuals honoured in the monument. Indeed, the modern British experience of commemorating the war dead, especially of the First World War, for which entire brigades were recruited from single communities, offers something of the sense of commemoration found in ancient Greece, where an athlete was competing not merely for his own

17

18

glory, but to advance the fame of his city. The strong sense of belonging to a community, of which membership was in practice very exclusive, explains why so many of the individual Greeks who have left a record of their names described themselves not only by name but also by citizenship, and in some cases also by ethnic origin. To press the modern military analogy a little further, just as the unknown soldier represents an idealised view of personal valour and other soldierly qualities, so the Greek athlete represents the acme of sporting achievement. Only those who had won three Olympic victories had their personal features recorded in commemorative statues (Pliny, *Natural History*, XXXV, 16).

Surviving references to individuals in classical portraits are not numerous, as few original bronze statues and bases survive intact. An exception is the bronze statue of a charioteer found at Delphi, dedicated in 478 or 474 BC. The restored text on the base reads: 'Polyzales, son of

17 Above left *Seated marble figure identified on the inscribed throne as Chares, ruler of Teichioussa in Caria; made about 575 BC. One of a series of figures set up along the sacred way leading from the city of Miletus to the oracular sanctuary of Apollo at Didyma.*

18 Above *The* Discobolus *(discus-thrower); Roman marble version of a lost Greek original made by the sculptor Myron about 450 BC. Myron has captured here the moment of tension before the throw.*

19

19 *Bronze statue of a charioteer, dedicated at Delphi after a victory in 478 or 474 BC by Polyzales, owner of the chariot and tyrant of Gela (Sicily). The unnamed charioteer wears a long* chiton *(tunic) with shoulder cords and a belt to prevent it from billowing in the wind. He holds the remains of reins; fragments of the chariot, horse-legs and tail were found with the figure.*

Deinomenes, victorious with his [chariot] horses dedicated me; make him prosper, honoured Apollo.' The charioteer is not personally named; the honour goes to the wealthy horse-owner Polyzales of Gela in Sicily, who paid for the statue. More common, though, are classical bronze figures long since removed from their bases, such as the fine head of a Libyan found at Cyrene in eastern Libya, and bases from which the statues they once supported have long been lost.

The earliest statues of named individuals were set up, like other forms of monumental sculpture, in religious sanctuaries and cemeteries. In a sanctuary, such statues mostly represented wealthy and powerful people who had made substantial dedications to the deity or who had held costly office; another class of statues commemorates those who, like the soldiers honoured in modern times, lost their lives prematurely in the service of their community. Most of these figures are not of great interest for the art of portraiture but they represent an important phase in the development of the idea of representing the individual. The images in sanctuaries are first recorded in the seventh century BC; the funerary monuments at the start of the sixth. These dates may of course reflect only the accident of preservation of monumental figures in stone and there may well have existed earlier representations in less durable materials such as wood or ivory, of which we now know nothing. However, even the earliest commemorations may be quite complex. The idea of portraying significant groups or pairs of figures, a notion of great importance to Hellenistic Greek and Roman portraiture, had evidently developed by this time in Greece – indeed, it had already enjoyed a long currency in dynastic Egypt. An early Greek example is offered by the so-called Geneleos Group, in which the figures were arranged in various comfortable poses

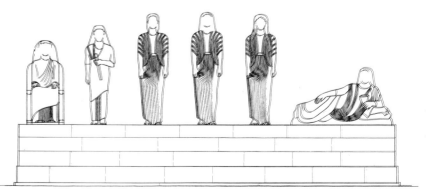

20 *Reconstructed drawing of the Geneleos Group, found in the sanctuary of Hera on Samos and made about 560–550 BC. The group takes its name from the signature 'Geneleos made us' on the legs of Phileia, the seated figure on the left. The next figure is probably a boy, the third an unnamed girl, while the fourth and fifth are named Philippe and Ornithe. The dedicator, whose name only survives in part, reclines on cushions.*

on their plinth, which was dedicated in the sanctuary of Hera on the eastern Aegean island of Samos. The precise significance of the order is now lost to us, but it is likely that the group represents a family, who were benefactors of the sanctuary. From left to right the figures are (seated) Phileia, whose legs are inscribed 'Geneleos made us'; a boy, an unnamed girl, a girl named Philippe, a girl named Ornithe and a man whose name is only partially preserved, reclining on cushions. The attraction of the group is illustrated by the recent use of the figures in an advertising campaign by the Greek Tourist Office, inviting British tourists to, as it were, join the party.

Figures of youths and girls, the *kouroi* and *korai* of which many examples survive, sometimes served as a memorial to the deceased (for example, the statue of Kroisos, set up about 530 BC at Anavysos in Attica to mark the grave of a youth fallen in battle), but sometimes appeared in sanctuaries, where their interpretation is not always so clear.

Some individuality – or at least a hint of social status – may be gleaned from certain archaic images of the human figure, though it must be admitted that the conventional static poses do not help us to see the individual behind the smile. The so-called Rampin horseman or rider, set up on the Athenian Acropolis about 550 BC, is unusually distinctive among archaic representations of mortals. No inscribed name survives, and the boy's head is in the Louvre while his torso and horse remain in Athens. The figure's distinction lies in its pose: instead of looking straight ahead, the head is turned sharply away from the rigidly frontal torso as if to invite the viewer's gaze. Having thus captured the viewer's attention, the rider offers for detailed contemplation an elaborate and unusual hairstyle. Finds of more fragments suggest that the Rampin rider was one of a group of two figures, their horses turning inwards and their heads turning out. The survivor's crown is of wild celery, representing a victory won in the Isthmian or Nemean games. Thus the Rampin rider was in life a competitor seeking the attention of an audience and, despite the chronological gulf between them, the effect of this figure on the viewer may be compared with that of the second-century AD orator also from Athens (cover), whose head is similarly turned to seek the viewer's attention.

Some modern viewers may be concerned that the identity of some unnamed archaic figures remains obscure and could even be mythical.

21 Opposite *Cast of the 'Rampin rider'. The head is in Paris and the rest of the group in Athens, where the sculptures were found on the Athenian Acropolis and made about 550 BC. The wreath of wild celery recalls a victory in the Isthmian or Nemean games.*

21

The Greeks did not trouble over such distinctions: they accepted the historicity of Homer when they created his portrait several centuries after the *Iliad* and the *Odyssey* were composed. The Greek lack of interest in distinguishing between mortal and immortal figures is reflected in the ambiguity and idealisation with which they represented the human figure. Who is portrayed in the imposing bronzes found in the sea near Riace: heroes of legend or distinguished mortals?

A particularly interesting and tantalising instance of the representation of mortals in late archaic art concerns a group of vase-painters, dubbed the Pioneers by modern scholars, who were active in the last quarter of the sixth century BC. The name given to the group reflects their interest in experimenting with complicated poses and views in the newly developed red-figure technique of vase-painting. The Pioneers exploited the technique of red-figure (in which the figures, in red, are reserved in the clay and the black painted around them) with evident panache and no little levity. Unexpectedly for a group of painters of possibly mixed origin and social class, they painted each other enjoying symposia (drinking parties) alongside the *kaloikagathoi*, literally the beautiful and good (for so they were described) youths of aristocratic families. Again, we may identify the vase-painters not from physical characteristics but only because they named themselves in their paintings; they also named other guests at the symposia, wrote mottoes or challenges to each other, and even allowed figures to speak like modern cartoon characters. A fragment of a mixing-bowl (*krater*) now in Munich shows a symposium scene by the most gifted painter of the group, Euphronios, in which the central figure, a youth reclining on a well-appointed *kline* (bed), is labelled Smikros, himself known from other compositions to be one of the Pioneers. A wine-cooler (*psykter*) now in the Getty Museum, Malibu, and thought to be by Smikros, portrays Euphronios as a beardless youth with the boy Leagros, in later life a distinguished general. Leagros was much admired for his beauty and was frequently painted, as was his son Glaukon. The family was of the cream of Athenian society. Why should Leagros consort with a painter, for such is the literal implication of this scene? And what social convention allowed the painter Smikros, whose name suggests a servile origin, to recline on a *kline*? If such inscriptions were found on monumental sculpture, we would be more confident about associating the figures and

their sumptuous setting with the identities offered by the inscriptions.

The society represented or mimicked in these paintings was transformed after the assassination of the tyrant Hipparchos by Harmodios, aided by his older lover Aristogeiton, in 514 BC. It is said that the motive for the killing was personal enmity, but the assassins were generally well regarded in the aftermath of the event, which effectively brought down the tyranny. Harmodios was killed immediately and Aristogeiton tortured before being put to death, but both assassins were subsequently honoured as heroes by the emerging democratic factions. Their group portrait, the first secular commemorative sculpture known to us in Greek art, was created by the distinguished sculptor Antenor about 500 BC or perhaps after the Battle of Marathon in 490. This group was removed by the Persian king Xerxes after the sack of Athens in 480

22 *Detail of a* psykter *(wine-cooler) attributed to the painter Smikros, about 510– 500 BC. Euphronios is here shown (left) dressed in a transparent cloak, leaning on a stick and reaching out to the aristocratic boy Leagros (right), described in an accompanying inscription as beautiful* (kalos). *Both figures are named.*

23 *Group showing Harmodios (right) and Aristogeiton (left) in the act of slaying the tyrant Hipparchus in 514 BC; Roman marble version, found at the villa of the emperor Hadrian at Tivoli, near Rome. The original group, now lost but known from a number of later versions, was dedicated in Athens about 475 BC.*

BC, but was replaced by a new bronze group made in 477/6 by Kritios and Nesiotes: it is known to us through Roman marble copies and, unusually, from late fifth- and fourth-century BC vase-paintings, coins and a representation in relief on a marble throne. There are many difficulties in interpreting the articulation of the later group, which is shown in various ways on the replicas. Fragments of the original plinth found in the Athenian Agora show there was only one base, not two as in the Roman version. The figures are quite strongly characterised, Aristogeiton as a sinewy mature man and Harmodios as a fleshy adolescent.

One of the friends of Leagros and his circle was the general and statesman Themistocles, a copy of whose portrait has survived in the

24 *Inscribed bust of the Athenian statesman and general Themistocles; Roman marble version of a lost original probably made after Themistocles' death about 460 BC.*

24 form of an inscribed herm (a head-and-shoulders portrait set upon a shaft) from the Roman port of Ostia. Some scholars have seen more of the later Roman Empire than of fifth-century Athens in this strikingly realistic image. Others see the turbulence of Themistocles' career, his stance as a revolutionary, his Thracian mother – anything that sets Themistocles apart from the fifth-century Athenian norm! The head certainly projects a strong character, and as such belongs to that rare class of portraits which are so individual as to transcend their time and thus prove difficult to place in context. It is surely reasonable to see, as many scholars have done, a visual resemblance between the head of Themistocles and the seer in the pediment of the Temple of Zeus at Olympia – a relationship which, if it has any chronological significance, implies a date of about 460 for the original portrait, which would then have been made, as might be expected, around the time of Themistocles' death. Such is the unusual power of this portrait that it has been made to stand for a phase of realism in fifth-century portraiture, or at least to represent an interest in portraying individual character as opposed to a loosely conceived ideal type. Many believe it to have been made in

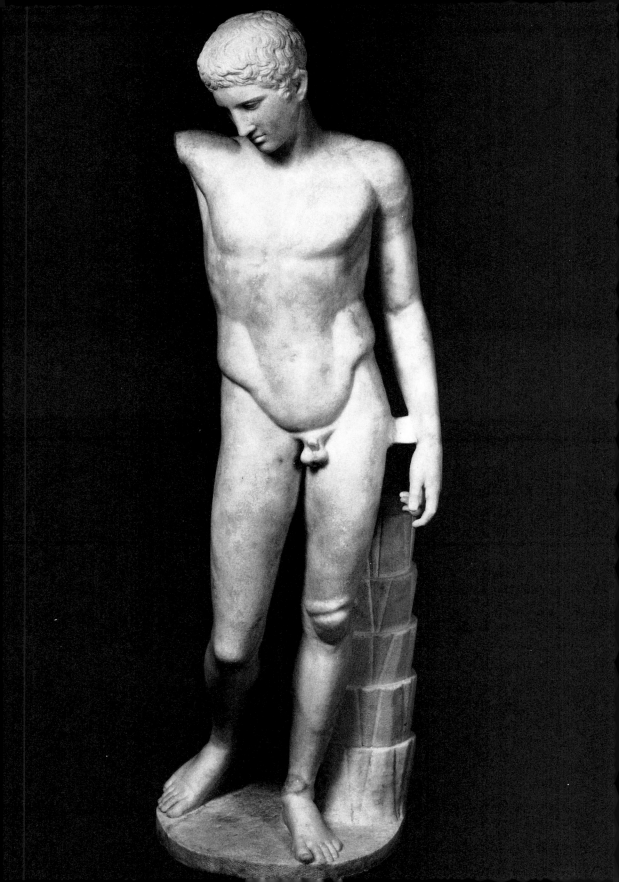

Magnesia, in western Asia Minor, where Themistocles fled after falling into disgrace at Athens. This may explain the apparent lack of concern for Athenian norms of depiction of the human figure, in which physical and moral perfection were emphasised at the expense of individual appearance and character.

It has been argued that the Argive sculptor Polykleitos – who was, with Pheidias, one of the most distinguished and influential artists of fifth-century Greece – developed a way of representing the aristocratic idea of *kaloskagathos* (physically beautiful and morally good) in a manner that was sympathetic to the democratic climate of mid-fifth-century Athens. Polykleitos devised a canon of proportions based upon the ideal human form; the canon is believed to be embodied in the Doryphoros, or spear-carrier, sculpted by Polykleitos and known to us from various Roman versions. The emergence of the Polykleitan ideal is thought to reflect a social levelling of the citizen body which is expressed in portraiture by the suppression of individual features and an emphasis on physical and moral perfection. The portrait of the Athenian political leader Pericles belongs in this tradition: it speaks of male maturity (signified by a full beard), physical strength and moral worth. The artist is said to have concealed his subject's unusually long head by adjusting the angle of the helmet. Though we know Pericles from Roman portraits in the form of herms, his original portrait was, like all classical Greek images, a full-length statue. It is easier to suppress individuality in whole figure portraits; the most powerful portraits are bust-length representations that make the viewer look at the head.

The conventions developed in Periclean Athens lasted a long time in Athenian funerary art and commemorative portraiture. Although the scenes on Athenian tombstones include tender and sometimes specific vignettes of family life, there are no individualised faces amongst the persons thus portrayed. Such 'democratic' anonymity was to be undermined in the fourth century BC by the growing popularity of portraits of poets and philosophers too individual to conform, and by the emergence of kingdoms on the margins of the Greek world whose courts patronised Greek artists and whose rulers were interested in creating a quite different image of themselves. Particularly prominent amongst those artists associated with the rise of portraits of individuals are the sculptors Lysippos (see chapter 4) and Demetrios of Alopeke, a sculptor working

25 Opposite *Marble statue of a youth; reduced scale Roman version of an original, now lost, made by the Greek sculptor Polykleitos about 450 BC.*

in bronze and active from about 400 to 360 BC. Demetrios is known from a series of signed bases and from literary references, including an amusing fantasy by the Roman satirist Lucian (*Philopseudes*, 18) on Demetrios' portrait of the Corinthian general Pellichos:

> 'When you came into the hall', he said, 'didn't you notice an absolutely lovely statue up there, by Demetrios the portraitist?'
>
> 'You surely don't mean the discus-thrower?'
>
> 'No, not that one, nor the Diadumenos [victorious athlete] or the Tyrannicides, but perhaps you saw the piece by the fountain with a pot belly, a bald head, half exposed by the fall of his cloak, with some of the hairs of his beard blown by the wind, and with prominent veins, just like the man himself, that's the one I had in mind: he's said to be Pellichos, the Corinthian general.'
>
> 'Good heavens', I said, 'I saw it to the right of the water-spout, wearing fillets and withered wreaths, the chest covered with gilded leaves.'
>
> 'I put on the gilded leaves myself', said Eukrates, 'when it cured me of the gout that was tormenting me every other day.'
>
> 'Really, is our good Pellichos a doctor too?', I said.
>
> 'Don't mock him', replied Eukrates, 'or before long the man will punish you. I know what power resides in that statue you make fun of. Don't you think that he can induce fevers in whomsoever he wishes, since he is also capable of sending them away?'
>
> 'May the image be gracious and kind, since he is so manful', I said.

The dialogue continues with an account of the statue singing and bathing at night, a fine satire on contemporary Roman belief in the power of portraiture.

CHAPTER 4

Portraits of Greeks in the Roman World

While the vast majority of original Greek portraits are lost to us, we may still follow the growing interest in the individual in the late classical and Hellenistic Greek world through the collections of portraits of famous Greeks made by Roman intellectuals and aesthetes to adorn their houses, libraries and gardens. In the late Republic and early Empire the city of Athens offered an attractive option for the further education of young male Romans of good family, such as the orator and statesman Cicero, who as a student in the 70s BC tried to save the house of the philosopher Epicurus from ruin. In his letters to Atticus, who in the 60s BC acted as his agent in Athens, purchasing works of art for the orator's villa at Tusculum, near Rome, Cicero reveals how his country house was furnished as a microcosm of the ancient seats of Athenian learning, the Academy of Plato and the Lycaeum of Aristotle. The rooms and garden of the villa were decorated with bronze portrait busts of Greek luminaries, set upon shafts of Pentelic marble in a deliberate evocation of the herms or boundary markers of classical Athens.

The bust or herm was to become a favourite form of portraiture amongst the Romans. The head was set on a tapering shaft, with stump-like arms and, in some cases, genitals carved in relief. Some portrait herms were inscribed with the name of the subject, and many were marked with letters indicating the order in which the herm-portraits were to be set. The introduction of portrait busts and herms of famous subjects long since deceased also reflected a change in the function of portraiture in the Hellenistic Greek and hellenised Roman world. Greek portraiture was originally intended to commemorate heroes and important figures in public life but, for Hellenistic and Roman connoisseurs,

portraits of famous Greeks of the classical period gained a new significance as emblems of a much-admired culture. It was neither appropriate
nor practical to install in a private library or dining-room a life-sized or
larger statue, of which only the head now represented those aspects of
character most important to the viewer.

The portrait of the charismatic philosopher Socrates, known to us in
some thirty surviving Roman versions of lost Greek prototypes, is one of
several fourth-century characterisations of brilliant individuals that
represent a decisive break with the idealised anonymity of fifth-century
Athenian representations of the human figure. The best-known version
of Socrates' portrait bears comparison with the work of the sculptor
Lysippos (active from about 370 to 305 BC), who was renowned for his
ability to capture the drama of individual character while accurately
observing specific details of personal appearance. The similarity of
Socrates' portrait to contemporary figures on Athenian grave reliefs
suggests that Lysippos created it late in his career, many decades after the
philosopher's execution in 399 BC. During and long after his lifetime,
Socrates' ugly physical appearance, sometimes compared to that of
Silenos, the drunken old companion of the wine-god Dionysos, was the
cause of comment. How could it be that such a noble and brilliant mind
lived within so undistinguished a body? The paradox presented considerable difficulties in contemporary Greece, where the notion of
physical perfection had held such a central position in fifth-century ideas
of the depiction of the human character. Only outsiders – barbarians, or
the disfigured or deformed – were shown with any degree of realism, and
that tended towards caricature. After Socrates' death, the scourge of the
Athenian political establishment came to be seen as an heroic figure,
representing an uncompromising truthfulness more profound than any
political expediency. Unease about Socrates' ungainly appearance was
resolved by the view that, just as the savage appearance of Silenos
concealed a divine spirit, so were the spiritual qualities of Socrates
embodied within his unworthy frame.

For the artist, there were practical remedies for physically imperfect
subjects. Just as the sculptor of Pericles' portrait had concealed the
elongated skull of the great statesman within a specially tilted helmet, so
the Lysippan version of Socrates' portrait favourably modified the
philosopher's inelegant appearance by heightening the brow and accen-

tuating the bone structure. Anticipating later Hellenistic fashions, the mouth was left slightly open and the hair and beard were softly contoured. The favourable manipulation of physical appearance, by no means restricted to the subjects of classical Athenian portraiture, is in a sense comparable to the reverse process of caricature, in that both allow the artist freedom to recreate the identity of a subject.

A group of portrait heads, apparently intended to be set on herms and found to the south of Rome by the Via Appia, may serve as an illustration of the Roman passion for portraits of famous Greeks. They include a portrait of the philosopher Antisthenes, described by Lucian of Samosata, writing in the second century AD, as having 'a halo of beard, eyebrows an inch above their place, superiority in his air, a look that might storm heaven, locks waving in the wind – a very Boreas or Triton from [the classical painter] Zeuxis' brush'. A pupil of Socrates who fought alongside his master at the battle of Tanagra in 426 BC, Antisthenes founded the Cynic school of philosophy at the Gymnasium of Kynosarges in Athens. It was said that his harsh regime attracted few pupils.

Three other portraits in this group represent Epicurus (341–270 BC), hugely popular amongst the Roman intelligentsia, and two of his

26 *Two marble portraits from a group found near the Via Appia, south of Rome: on the left the philosopher Epicurus (342/1–271/0 BC), founder of a successful and influential school teaching that freedom from pain and peace of mind represent the greatest good, for which virtue is a necessary precondition; and on the right the founder of the Cynic school of philosophy Antisthenes (c. 450–370 BC). A pupil of Socrates, Antisthenes was interested in endurance and harshness. The portrait suggests an elderly man of strong personality and vision but dishevelled appearance.*

followers, Metrodorus of Lampsacus (331–278 BC) and Hermarchus of Mytilene (340–*c*.270 BC), who inherited Epicurus' library. The portraits of Antisthenes and Epicurus appear to be the work of one sculptor, while those of Metrodorus and a poet, thus far unidentified, have sharply chiselled features reminiscent of classical Athenian work. The nose of the portrait of Metrodorus has been cut off in a deliberate act of mutilation. Sadly, nothing is recorded of the original arrangement of this group.

Archaeological evidence for the setting of Greek portraits mixed with other sculptures in a Roman context is offered by the Villa of the Papyri at Herculaneum on the Bay of Naples. The villa takes its name from some 2,000 papyri discovered during exploration of the site in the mid-eighteenth century. Of 342 unrolled papyri, only 24 are Latin; the rest are Greek, and largely concerned with the works of the Epicurean philosopher Philodemus of Gadara (Palestine), a dull but successful populariser of a wide range of Greek works, active about the middle of the first century BC. A similar dominance of Greek figures, among which may be counted several portraits of Epicurus, appears in the sculptures recovered from the excavated part of the site, where the ratio of Greeks to Romans is in the order of 15:1. It is not out of the question that an equivalent library of Latin works remains to be discovered, and that our picture of the assemblage of portraits is distorted by partial recovery and poor standards of excavation and recording. Unquestionable, however, is the milieu of the refined and hellenised Roman intellectual, the owner evidently a follower of Epicurus. Most of the sculptures may be dated in the last quarter of the first century BC, in the early years of the reign of the first emperor Augustus (27 BC–AD 14). Several of them are thematically related, and it may be argued that some are the product of the same workshop.

Within the villa, the sculptures were disposed around a colonnaded court or peristyle, and in various rooms opening off the peristyle, including a hall (*atrium*) and a connecting salon (*tablinum*); the latter led to a large colonnaded garden (*xystos*) used for strolling and cultured conversation, a feature of Greek philosophical schools here agreeably fitted with a pool and pergola. The sculptures fall into three groups: portraits, both of Greek philosophers or men of letters and of Hellenistic Greek kings and queens (the royal portraits are perhaps unexpected, but serve to emphasise the position of leading men of the late Republic and early Empire as the effective heirs to the rulers of the Hellenistic Greek world); severely classicising works, falling well within the bounds of contemporary taste; and, lastly, Campanian garden sculpture of the sort known from Pompeii and other sites in the region.

Although archaeological evidence for their original placement is lost, the portraits from the villa were discovered in groups which, taken together, tell a story. There is much scholarly argument over the identification of some of the unnamed figures, and still more over the interpretation of the arrangement as a whole. Thus the sculptures displayed in the square peristyle have recently been interpreted as the nucleus of the collection, representing both intellectual and physical perfection, a very Greek notion, with portraits identified as Pythagoras and Empedocles embodying the former, while versions of the spear-carrier (Doryphoros) of Polykleitos and the Amazon of Pheidias represented the latter. The group of statues in the rectangular peristyle, perhaps intended as a *gymnasium*, may be taken to represent private life (*res privata* or *otium*, an essential requirement of the Roman nobility and clearly necessary to philosophical contemplation), contrasted with *res publica* or *negotium*, the burdensome duties of public life.

Epic poetry was represented by a portrait of Homer, by an inscribed herm of Panyassis of Halicarnassus and (the identification is less certain)

27

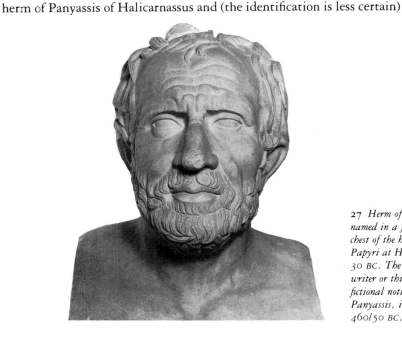

27 *Herm of Panyassis of Halicarnassus, named in a faded painted inscription on the chest of the herm; found in the Villa of the Papyri at Herculaneum and made about 30 BC. The representation of a balding writer or thinker with anxious expression is a fictional notion of the personal appearance of Panyassis, invented long after his death in 460/50 BC.*

by a portrait of Antimachus of Colophon (both epic poets of the fifth century BC); satirical poetry by portraits identified as Bion of Borysthenes (in the region of Olbia, on the Black Sea coast) and Menippus of Gadara (Palestine), both active in the early third century BC. These were the only branches of Greek literature considered by the Romans to have a social and moral function. Indeed, a moralising tendency was typical of early imperial attitudes to private collections of art, as Augustus crushed the competitive parading of individual wealth typical of the late Republic.

The commanding personalities of Socrates and of his admirer Alcibiades retained the interest of intellectuals into late antiquity. Both feature in a remarkable cycle of late Roman portraits recently discovered at Aphrodisias in Caria (south-west Asia Minor). At least part of the group was composed of paired portraits of teacher and pupil, appropriately designed to decorate the court of a philosophical school, a more public context than that of the country seats of the Roman nobility of the late Republic and early Empire. Besides Socrates and Alcibiades there appear the great Aristotle and his most distinguished pupil Alexander the Great of Macedon. The interests of the Aphrodisian school were evidently wide-ranging, for the early classical lyric poet Pindar was also 16 portrayed here, as were the mathematician and cosmologist Pythagoras, who emigrated from Samos to found a religious community at Croton in southern Italy in the late sixth century BC, and his distant disciple, the early Roman imperial miracle-worker Apollonius of Tyana in Cappadocia. More recent luminaries and contemporary figures were also included but they are unnamed and their identity is now unknown to us.

The portraits from Aphrodisias are among the most distinguished versions of classical Greek images to be created in later antiquity; many more Roman versions of Greek philosopher portraits are known in various media and from sites remote in time and place from classical Athens. A group of sixty-three stone portrait herms was recovered from an imperial villa of the later fourth century AD at Welschbillig (near Trier, Germany). The herms decorated the balustrade of a large pool (*piscina*), and included images of such distinguished Greeks as Socrates, the historian Thucydides and the orator Demosthenes, along with images of Macedonian kings, Roman emperors and even Greek philosophers of the Roman period with their pupils. Here too there is some evidence for the pairing of portraits representing opposing or associated ideas which is familiar in collections of portraits from other Roman sites.

Images of classical Greek personalities even formed a part of the late Roman interior decorator's repertoire: a mosaic pavement from a villa at Sparta in the Greek Peloponnese offers the only complete, securely identified portrait to survive of Alcibiades. Images of the Seven Sages were painted on tavern walls at Ostia, the port of Rome, in the early second century AD. Their names and cities of origin were carefully inscribed in Greek beside each portrait, while above the figures, in earthily scatalogical Latin, is written their advice on combating the problems of irregular digestion. At Kenchreai, the port of Corinth, late antique portraits of Greek philosophers were made on glass panels, forerunners of the stained-glass window portraits of saints familiar from Christian churches of more recent date. These and many more surviving examples illustrate the continued strength of the long-standing Roman interest in Greek culture. More is known of the late antique portraits,

IV
28

29

28 *Painted portrait of Cheilon of Sparta (Lacedaemon), one of the Seven Sages. Cheilon, who lived about 560 BC, is shown seated in a position of authority. A man of few words greatly revered for his wisdom, Cheilon was honoured as a hero of Sparta. This painting decorated a tavern at Ostia, the port of Rome. Cheilon's name and origin are given in Greek, and above and below is advice in Latin on how to combat indigestion.*

29 *Roman mosaic pavement found at Cologne. On entering the room, the visitor saw the cynic Diogenes (414–323 BC) in the centre. To the left are Cleoboulus (one of the Seven Wise Men), Socrates and Plato; to the right Sophocles, Aristotle and Cheilon (see fig. 28).*

because they are more visible in the archaeological record, and because they have a particular vigour, due perhaps to their creation at a time of tension between those who sought to preserve pagan traditions and those who had embraced Christianity, from the fourth century AD the official religion of the Roman Empire. It is also clear from surviving late Roman portraits of Greek philosophers that, although artists felt free to modify the form of the portrait, most were evidently familiar with the classical

Greek types, which had been transmitted in recognisable form over the better part of a millennium.

From the Villa of the Papyri to the school of Aphrodisias we may follow the Roman intellectuals' respect and even passion for classical Greek culture. Due to the enthusiasm of Roman scholars, the portraits of several of the most distinguished men and women of classical Greek antiquity survived the collapse of the political system in which their subjects played so great a role, and even the rise of Christianity.

30

30 *Marble head of the 'Pseudo-Seneca', a famous personality of whom over forty portraits survive. The head represents an old man of strong character and evident experience of suffering. His identity remains uncertain, but the head may represent the poet Hesiod, much associated in antiquity with Homer. When first discovered, the portrait was wrongly thought to represent the Roman philosopher Seneca.*

CHAPTER 5

Greek Portraits of Rulers

I n the Greek world, images of rulers first appear at the geographical margins, in such representations as the (now headless) statue of Chares, ruler of Teichioussa in Caria (south-west Asia Minor) in the sixth century BC, or images of Aristoteles, king of Cyrene in Libya in the mid-fifth century, and on coins of Kharei, dynast of Xanthus in Lycia towards the end of that century.

It is worth examining Lycia and its neighbour Caria in greater detail. These regions were part of the Persian empire, but lay so far from the seat of power that the Athenians gained control of Lycia for some of the fifth century BC. The area is often described by art historians as one of cross-cultural influence between Greece in the west and Persia in the east. While both Greek and Persian styles and motifs abound in Lycian art,

31 Silver stater with a representation of a bearded dynast, probably Kharei, dressed in a Persian tiara. About 420–400 BC.

32 Map of the Hellenistic Greek world showing the geographical extent of the former Persian Empire.

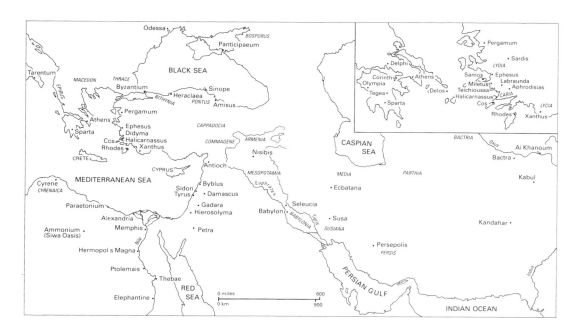

33 *A scene of diplomacy from the Nereid Monument, built about 380 BC, probably to commemorate the dynast Arbinnas of Xanthus, Lycia. A figure, probably a satrap (Persian governor), seated beneath a parasol with armed guards behind him, receives a delegation of bearded men in Greek dress, perhaps orators who plead their city's cause.*

the unique local character of Lycian monumental sculpture deserves serious consideration. All surviving Lycian ruler portraits date from the two periods of Persian rule, from 546 to 470 BC and from about 400 to 360 BC. The rulers of Lycia are portrayed as strong individuals, many of whom did well for their cities by conducting favourable negotiations with the Great King of Persia or with satraps controlling wider regions of western Asia Minor. The city politician who gains favours for his community at court is a recurrent figure in Greek and Roman portraiture, a motif that underlines the importance of the orator, who in antiquity was often a highly influential politician. Portraits of local dynasts on Lycian coins, which are the earliest images of living rulers to survive from the Greek world, were intended to remind people (especially soldiers who received the coins as pay) of the independent identity of the Lycian dynast and his territory. Tenacious and even suicidal devotion to independence marks all of Lycia's ancient history, and is a likely reason for the early appearance of ruler portraits in this region.

In the 360s BC the alliances between Lycian cities, which were never strong, collapsed in the face of the growing power of a neighbouring dynast, Mausolus of Caria. The monument commissioned to recall the life of Mausolus has given us the modern term 'mausoleum'. The exact form of Mausolus' tomb at Halicarnassus is the subject of much scholarly dispute, but it is known from literary descriptions and from the surviving remains to have had a stepped podium, on which were arranged marble statues illustrating life at Mausolus' court. As portrayed on the Mausoleum, the royal Carian lifestyle was unexceptional by regal standards of any time: Mausolus and his court hunted, received important guests and missions, performed religious ceremonies and stood in a meaningful order (now, alas, no longer clear to us) between grand fluted columns. The tomb of Mausolus had enormous influence on subsequent generations, and was described by the Romans with great admiration. The quality of the sculpture was considered outstanding: four of the foremost Greek sculptors of the day – Scopas, Leochares, Timotheos and Bryaxis – were commissioned to work on the monument. The free-standing painted figures of Pentelic and Parian marble imported from Greece were set off against a background of bluish-grey stones used to clad the podium and for much of the architectural decoration. The influence of the Mausoleum, particularly of the arrangement of the portrait statues, is certainly visible in later Roman monuments, such as the Library of Celsus at Ephesus, erected in the second century AD and also used as a tomb, and the fountain of Herodes Atticus at Olympia in Greece.

v

12

The Mausoleum is said to have been commissioned by Mausolus' sister-queen Artemisia, and was completed after her death by the Greek sculptors working 'for their own glory', as the Roman writer the elder Pliny has it (*Natural History*, XXXVI, XXX–XXXI); it is possible, however, that Mausolus' successor, his brother Idreus, also had a hand in the monument's completion. Idreus is a figure of some importance to the later history of commemorative portraiture: he was the first in the Greek world to put his name on the architrave of a temple, one of several buildings given to the sanctuary of Zeus at Labraunda, inland from the Carian capital of Halicarnassus, and he also patronised the most important religious sanctuaries of mainland Greece; monuments to him and his sister-queen Ada survive at Tegea in Arcadia and at Delphi. In these matters Idreus was a precursor of many later Hellenistic Greek kings and Roman grandees.

34

Despite their efforts at patronage of old Greece, the Carian rulers were soon eclipsed by the growth of a new military super-power, Macedon. Living as they did on the edge of Greece, the Macedonians were keen to show themselves part of the Greek world, whose superior culture was the object of admiration amongst most royal courts of the day. It was Alexander's achievement as a young man with an extraordinary sense of purpose to bring Greek culture to all the lands formerly under Persian

34 *Marble relief from the sanctuary of Athena at Tegea (Arcadia, southern Greece), made about 340 BC. The Carian god Zeus Labraundus is flanked by Ada (left), wife of Idrieus (right), brother of and successor to Mausolus. Each figure is named in the margin above.*

domination. Thus was created, by military conquest with an attendant cultural programme, the Hellenistic world which stretched from Greece to Mesopotamia and from the Black Sea to Egypt.

Alexander, who died unexpectedly young of a fever in 323 BC, was said by Roman writers to have been aware of the need to project a good image, appointing to his court those artists he considered most competent at portraying his character. The late Roman portrait of Alexander from Aphrodisias in Caria may reflect an original made in his lifetime which showed him as more ferocious than the (to modern eyes) rather pathetic images made after his death, when he was declared a god. His cult was founded in Alexandria, the site of his tomb, by Ptolemy, one of the most successful of his generals. The effect of the cult was to fossilise a romantic image of the young Alexander which one suspects had little to do with his actual life. The liveliest and most convincing images of him are the 'man of action' scenes such as the battle with Darius at the Issus, the painting brilliantly recreated in a mosaic made about 100 BC for a large house at Pompeii. Alexander, the fallen Persian prince in the centre and Darius are all portraits, as are, most likely, one or two companions of

Alexander who appear on horseback by his right elbow. Alexander is shown without his helmet so he may be easily recognised, a device repeated in many ancient battle scenes with less distinguished participants.

Alexander always appeared beardless, though with long flowing hair (he was, after all, a pupil of the philosopher Aristotle) and sideburns. The lack of a beard marked his youth at the time of his conquests rather than his personal appearance at the time of his death at the age of thirty-two. Many of his successors copied Alexander's appearance, though they were not necessarily qualified to do so by age. Before they developed their own images, however, they put portraits of Alexander on their coins in order to strengthen their connections with him and thus to legitimise shaky positions as successors to a divided and contested kingdom. The three areas to emerge as major powers after the division of Alexander's empire were Egypt, controlled by the Ptolemies, Syria, run by the Seleucids, and Macedon itself, which controlled Greece. Of the minor kings, the most important, in the early days at least, were the Attalids of Pergamon, who came to control a substantial part of western Asia Minor.

35

35 *Silver coin minted by Ptolemy 1 of Egypt, showing Alexander the Great of Macedon wearing the elephant's scalp linking him to the wine-god Dionysos, conqueror of the east.*

The purposes and forms of Hellenistic royal portraits have received much scholarly attention in recent years, and are as a result reasonably well understood, though there remain intractable problems in dating individual images. The kings were most often represented naked (not of course shocking to the followers of traditional Greek culture), usually standing with a spear or staff. They might otherwise be shown standing in armour or on horseback – if the latter, then again in armour or dressed in a cloak and tunic. Unlike Roman emperors, they never appeared standing in civilian dress, for civic life was not their concern.

From the end of the fourth century BC, royal portraiture became of central concern to the Greeks, and many portraits were dedicated by the Greek cities which now came under Macedonian rule. A royal statue was given as the highest point in a range of civic honours awarded to individuals. To the Greeks, the erection of a royal portrait statue represented a means of dealing with a new form of power of which they had no previous experience. A statue might be voted by a community in expectation of a royal gift; if the community were lucky, their embassy informing the king of the impending honour might return home with the means to pay for it. The community was able, especially by the means of instituting a cult of the king, to buy his personal protection for the city and its inhabitants. Thus ruler cults in the Greek cities were of individual kings, not dynasties; they were set in sacred enclosures or in existing public buildings such as *gymnasia* or council chambers, which were not usually provided with a special temple for this purpose.

Hellenistic kings also instituted cults of themselves and especially of their ancestors. These cults were mostly confined to the royal capitals (part of the acropolis of Pergamon in western Asia Minor, the seat of the Attalid dynasty, is thought to have been exclusively reserved for their statues), to sanctuaries open to all Greek communities, such as those at Delos, Delphi and Olympia, and to other sites within their kingdoms. The purpose of cult statues was to publicise the relationships of present kings to past rulers and to proclaim their exalted status. The dedications made at Delos are of particular interest, for they speak of rivalry for control of the Aegean and of a decline in the number of royal portraits coinciding with the rise of Roman influence in the region in the second century BC. Members of royal courts were sometimes included in such groups, as were minor members of the royal family.

36 *Marble head of Mithradates VI, King of Pontus (112–63 BC), wearing a lion's scalp; perhaps a later version of a lost original made early in his reign. The lion's scalp is intended to compare Mithradates with Alexander the Great, who wears the lion's scalp in some of his coin portraits (see fig. 35).*

The Ptolemies in Egypt and the Seleucids in Syria organised official cults under centralised control. These were to become of critical importance for the workings of the Roman imperial cult which, like Hellenistic ruler cults, was simply added to existing religious ritual. Often the kings were likened to deities, whose insignia they wore. It is not often remembered that part of the text of the famous Rosetta stone, now in the British Museum and best known for its pivotal role in the decipherment of Egyptian hieroglyphs, is concerned with honours voted to Ptolemy V after he had restored order to the countryside and given benefactions to the temples of the old gods (lines 39–42):

> A statue [*eikon*, thus a large figure in hard stone] is to be set up in every temple in the most prominent place; it shall be called Ptolemy the Defender of Egypt, and beside him shall stand the principal god of the temple presenting to him the weapon of victory; these [statues] shall be made in the native Egyptian manner and the priests shall worship the statues three times a day and put on them the sacred dress, and perform the customary rites as for the other gods at festivals and religious

assemblies. A gilded shrine with a statue [a small wooden effigy] of King
Ptolemy is to be set up in every temple and is to be placed in the
innermost sanctuaries together with the other shrines, and in the great
religious assemblies in which the shrines are carried in procession, the
shrine of the god manifest and beneficent shall also be carried. . . .

Statues of his or her ancestors were used to stress a ruler's legitimacy and
often represented a quasi-divine lineage, usually produced on the ruler's
initiative. The most striking surviving example is offered by the groups
carved in the limestone of Nemrud Dağ in Commagene (eastern Asia
Minor) by the king Antiochus I shortly before the Roman conquest of the
region between 70 and 30 BC. The figures were set on terraces on either
side of the royal tomb. Two apparently identical lines of forebears were
represented, demonstrating the two supposed lines of royal descent from
Achaemenid Persia and the Seleucids of Syria. The lines go back to the
fourth century BC and include mythical representations as well as some
curious imaginative characterisations, such as Xerxes or Darius in a
fictional dressing-gown and tiara with a rolled peak, reflecting an
entirely Greek notion of Persian royal dress.

There are many difficulties in dating Hellenistic royal portraits,
which do not fall within so neat a typology as images of Roman
emperors, the latter created within a much more coherent political and
geographical framework. Not the least of our problems is the disap-
pointing survival rate: there are over 250 surviving statues of the Roman
emperor Augustus (who is, admittedly, exceptional in this respect) and
at least 100 for each emperor of the second century AD, but only about
120 for all the Hellenistic kings from Alexander to Augustus. In the
Hellenistic period most statues continued to be made, as they had been
in the classical period, of bronze, and, when no longer of interest, they
fell into the melting pot along with all other bronzes surplus to
requirements. Furthermore, unlike Greek writers and philosophers,
Hellenistic kings were with few exceptions not popular subjects for the
Roman copyist.

With Roman ruler portraiture we are often able successfully to relate a
sculptured image to a named figure on a coin, but in Hellenistic royal
portraits there is no such close rapport between statues, which served one
purpose, and images on coins, which served another. In archaic and

classical times, it had been the practice of the Greek cities to show a patron deity of the city on the obverse of the coin, and a city legend on the reverse. The coin illustrated its source, and the designs also provided a guarantee of stable value. With few exceptions, no heads of monarchs were put on coins until after Alexander's death; he appeared on coins of Ptolemy of Egypt by 318 BC and on coins of Lysimachus of Pergamon and Seleucus of Syria. By 306/5, when it was no longer possible to pretend that Alexander's empire had survived as a unity, the rulers began to put their own heads on the coinage. By this time Alexander was the subject of a divine cult, but portraits on coins asserted the independent status of local dynasts. Coin portraits were used according to local circumstances; they were of little significance in Macedon, for example, where there was no problem of royal legitimacy nor a cult of the ruler. In Egypt, the Ptolemies showed portraits of the founder of the dynasty on silver coinage; later kings occasionally appeared on gold and bronze issues. The Seleucids showed successive reigning monarchs, as did the Attalids from 262 to 133 BC. Smaller unstable kingdoms used coins to pay armies; it was important for the soldiers to know who was in charge (this was also a significant factor in the development of portraiture on Roman coins of the late Republic).

Royal portraits appeared on archive sealings too, where impressions taken from royal intaglios were used to close papyrus rolls. Several

37 *Heads of statues of a bearded man (left) with a wreath of laurel hung with beads of acorns, dated to 475–450 BC, and a man with sideburns (right), dated to the first century BC; from the sanctuary of Apollo at Idalion, Cyprus. The heads illustrate the striking change in the representation of individuals following the imposition of Ptolemaic Greek rule in Cyprus.*

38 Below left *Faience jug with a full-length portrait of Queen Arsinoë II of Egypt (c. 275–270 BC). The jug is inscribed with a dedication to the queen, who pours a libation in front of an altar. The queen carries a* cornucopia *brimming with the fruits of Egypt. An influential ruler, Arsinoë was the first queen to be worshipped as a goddess (of good fortune) during her lifetime.*

39 Below right *Bronze bust recut from a statuette of a naked diademed ruler. The subject is perhaps Ptolemy IV, Philopator of Egypt (221–203 BC), but it is difficult to make a certain identification as successive early Ptolemaic rulers were portrayed with similar personal features.*

hundred late Ptolemaic portraits on seals have survived from Edfu, 130 with portraits of kings, 26 with queens, and 12 with multiple portraits. The images are cruder versions of those appearing on coin dies. The cult of the Ptolemies was instrumental in influencing radical changes of form in local portraiture in areas under Ptolemaic control such as Cyprus and Cyrenaica. The cult also saw the production of relatively inexpensive images of Ptolemaic rulers. Portraits of queens survive on faience jugs, where applied reliefs show the queen pouring a libation before an altar. The inscription refers to royal good fortune. The faience jugs appear to be copies of vessels of precious metal used in the cult of both dead and living queens. Terracotta and bronze statuettes were also made in some quantity. The media used for small-scale portraits thus ranged from the very grand, such as cameos in precious or semiprecious stones, made for ministers, friends and supporters, and sometimes set in the crowns worn by the priests of the royal cult, through silver and faience vessels to rings worn as symbols of allegiance, or even to bone or ivory gaming counters. In all these media the portraits were highly idealised – icons in the

37

38

39

modern sense rather than true representations. They are therefore difficult to recognise individually and thus to date.

40 Ptolemaic rulers generally wore the diadem, a flat band of cloth tied at the back of the head, the ends being allowed to fall on the shoulders. The origin of the diadem is controversial, but it is thought to commemorate spear-won land – specifically, the lands won in conquest by Alexander the Great. It thus came to symbolise the heritage of Alexander, but was also linked with the wine-god Dionysos, who wore a band low on the forehead. The Romans avoided it, preferring the more martial and less regal laurel wreath, at least until Constantine moved his court to Constantinople in the fourth century AD.

Portraits of Hellenistic rulers were inevitably influenced by the growth of two new super-powers, Rome in the west and Parthia in the east. As Rome conquered the Greek world, civic portraiture grew in importance in Greek lands, and we see in the first century BC the rise of

40 *Marble head from a statue of a diademed king, perhaps Ptolemy Apion (died 94 BC), who bequeathed his kingdom of Cyrenaica to the Romans. Found in the sanctuary of Apollo at Cyrene.*

portraits showing signs of a certain cultural confusion: it is not certain in 41,
every case whether the subject is a pro-Roman Greek or a philhellene
Roman.

Though Hellenistic ruler portraits are difficult to categorise and date,
they are of great significance in the development of images of rulers. The
Romans borrowed much from the practices of the kings, especially the
Ptolemaic rulers of Egypt. The notion of replicating portraits on objects
of personal but no great artistic significance, such as bronze finger-rings,
certainly passed to Rome from Alexandria, together with the recipe for a
bronze high in tin which may have been cheaper to produce. However,
although Roman rulers learned much from their Hellenistic predecessors, they rarely sought to look like Greek kings, preferring an image
either more reflective of traditional Roman virtues or derived from the
democratic notions of classical Athens.

41 *Marble portrait of a man shown in Roman style but
lacking the detailed recording of physical imperfections
characteristic of Roman verism. Found in Rhodes, the
portrait resembles coin images of Nicias of Cos, a local
ruler installed by Mark Antony about 44 to 30 BC.*

CHAPTER 6

The Imperial Image of Augustus

Like many public figures before and after him, the first emperor of Rome was concerned about his image. This much is clear from the known portraits of Augustus, though there are no surviving contemporary accounts of the process of selecting the form of his portrait or of the artists who devised it. We may imagine the power of portraiture in an age in which personal access to the emperor was of critical importance but remained for most of his subjects a dream. For many the statue in the temple or market-place, the effigy in the shrine at home, the head on the seal or the coin, were more than images: they represented the emperor in person. Thus we learn of records of state fastened to a statue of Julius Caesar in his Forum at Rome, of later imperial portraits used as places of asylum, and of appeals for justice being made to statues of the emperor.

With so much hope invested in them, imperial images became an easy target for disappointed subjects. Indeed, the process of *damnatio memoriae* (posthumous condemnation) of an unpopular emperor did not concern the repeal of his acts so much as the physical destruction of his images and of records of his name. The sense of betrayal and revenge is well conveyed by an unexpected source, that respectable senator the younger Pliny (*Panegyric*, 92, 4):

> It was our delight to dash those proud faces to the ground, to smite them with the sword and savage them with the axe as if blood and agony could follow from every blow. Our transports of joy, so long deferred, were unrestrained; all sought a form of vengeance in beholding those mutilated bodies, limbs hacked to pieces, and finally that baleful, fearsome visage cast into the fire to be melted down. . . .

Thus fell the portraits of the unloved emperor Domitian (AD 81–96). There are, of course, many modern examples of such violent feelings towards persons of authority who had disappointed the expectations invested in them. Eastern Europe offers a fine contemporary portfolio: opposite Gorky Park in Moscow an outdoor sculpture collection was expanded after the collapse of the Communist regime to include an exhibition entitled 'Activists of Totalitarianism'. Here lies Felix Dzerzhinsky, founder of the original version of the KGB, his effigy prostrate and paint-spattered after its ignominious removal from a commanding position in the centre of Moscow, a dramatic fall widely shown on Western European television. There, too, a broken head of Khrushchev, hauled from storage, and a once-proud statue of Stalin with his hand tucked inside his jacket in the familiar 'broken arm' posture.

In antiquity such mutilated images would have been recycled in the lime kiln, if marble and beyond hope of recutting, or melted down if bronze. Mutilation does not necessarily result from the ravages of time and the elements, or even from a 'natural' fall from a pedestal, an event that tends to result in a broken nose, lips and chin. Instances occur of barbaric punishments meted out to ancient images in imitation of the harsh justice accorded to criminals in real life: a bust of Germanicus Caesar, Augustus' step-grandson and in his day one of the most popular   42
members of the imperial family, has had the nose cut off, a cross chiselled in the forehead and an unsuccessful attempt made at cutting the throat.

Even Augustus was vulnerable. A fine bronze head, the eyes inlaid   VI
with glass and alabaster, comes from an over-life-sized statue of the emperor in military dress, deliberately decapitated by tribesmen from the kingdom of Meroe (southern Sudan) who in 25 and 24 BC raided Roman forts and settlements in upper Egypt. The tribesmen buried the head at Meroe under the steps of a temple of victory. On the steps over the head were paintings of bound prisoners, so that anyone walking into the temple would literally step on the head of Augustus and on those of the prisoners – a supreme insult. The interior wall of the temple was decorated with a painting of the king and regent queen of Meroe sacrificing to the god Amun, whose foot rests on a stool painted with bound prisoners kneeling in attitudes of support and submission. The figure on the left of the footstool is thought to be wearing a Roman legionary helmet, but it is not clear whether the painting refers directly

42 *Green basanite bust of Germanicus Caesar in military dress; said to be from Egypt and made about* AD 16–40. *The nose has been sliced off and a cross incised in the forehead: an attempt has been made to slit the throat. The damage was probably inflicted in late antiquity by Christians opposed to pagan imagery.*

to the raids of 25–24 BC, well known from literary sources, or whether it represents the global limits of Meroitic interests, from the Roman legionary in the north to the Ethiopian in the south, with two plump Ptolemaic Egyptian figures in between.

When complete, the bronze statue from Meroe had surely offered a powerful and awe-inspiring image of the first emperor of Rome. How much did it resemble Augustus in person? A description survives of the emperor's personal features, written a century after his death by the biographer Suetonius (*Augustus*, 79). The account is quite contradictory, suggesting a mixture of palace gossip with the more favourable aspects drawn perhaps from the surviving portraits of Augustus:

> Throughout his life his appearance was distinguished and graceful. He did not dress extravagantly and cared so little about his hair that several barbers worked furiously on it at the same time. His beard was either trimmed or shaved while he continued reading or writing. He had clear, bright eyes . . . few teeth, which were small and dirty . . . his hair was

yellowish and slightly curly, his eyebrows met and his nose jutted out
and then turned inwards. He was neither dark nor fair and was rather
short, but with well-proportioned limbs. On his body were spots,
birthmarks and callouses caused by excessive use of the strigil. . . . He
sometimes limped and suffered in general from a weak constitution. . . .
Unable to endure heat or cold, he always wore a hat outdoors and in
winter wore a woollen vest.

We may pass over the more distasteful aspects of Augustus' diseases and
disfigurements to observe a certain distance between the physical
qualities offered by the written description and the heroised presentation
of the emperor in his official images.

Some biographical detail may explain the transformation. Augustus
was born Gaius Octavius at Rome on 24 September 63 BC, of respectable
family; his father held public office and had recently remarried into the
patrician family of Julius Caesar (Octavian's mother Atia was Caesar's
niece). Gaius Octavius shot to prominence at the age of eighteen when
his great-uncle Julius Caesar was assassinated in March of 44 BC. Having
no legitimate son, Julius Caesar had in his will named Gaius Octavius as
his heir. The young man inherited a great name and a vast fortune. Being
heir to Caesar was his first political position, one greatly enhanced in 42
BC when Julius Caesar was declared a god. Gaius Julius Caesar, as he
styled himself, then enjoyed divine approval; two years later he began to
describe himself on his coins as 'son of the deified Julius'.

The earliest portraits of Octavian appeared on coins minted from 43
BC onwards to pay a client army loyal to him. The portrait on the coins
reminded the troops of the loyalty they owed their paymaster, while the
beard (here worn as a sign of vengeance or mourning) and the legend
around the edge of the coin spelled out the link with the murdered
Caesar. A few sculptured portraits probably representing the bearded
Octavian have survived from this period. One was discovered in the
Forum at Arles in southern France, a colony founded by Julius Caesar
and later the centre of a cult of Augustus.

In 42 BC Octavian founded a triumvirate 'to put the state in order'
with two experienced politicians, Mark Antony and Lepidus. The
uneasy alliance lasted about eight years, until Lepidus was dismissed in
36 BC and hostilities grew between Octavian and Antony, fuelled by

43 *Coin portraits of
Octavian: (a) bearded in
mourning or revenge for the
murder of Caesar, 38 BC;
(b) in a style influenced by
the portraits of Hellenistic
kings, about 33 BC.*

a

b

43a

I **Above** *Bronze head of a bearded man with a thin fillet in his hair, perhaps the Athenian tragic poet Sophocles (c.496–406 BC). The portrait clearly represents an elderly man and may evoke Sophocles' refutation of a formal charge of senility brought against him by his son Iophon.*

II **Above right** *Marble head from a statue of a woman; from Carthage and made about AD 100. The artist has reproduced the intricate hairstyle with consummate illusionistic skill. The elaboration of the hairstyle is sharply contrasted with the plainness of the woman's face and unplucked eyebrows.*

III **Right** *Bronze head of a Libyan horseman, found in the Temple of Apollo at Cyrene (eastern Libya) and made in the fourth century BC. The young man has curly hair, prominent cheekbones and full lips, characteristic features of the Berber peoples who have inhabited Cyrenaica since remote antiquity. Fragments of a horse were said to have been found with the head, but no accompanying inscription has survived.*

IV **Above** *Inscribed panel portrait of Alcibiades from a Roman mosaic pavement found in Sparta. This is the only surviving extant portrait of Alcibiades (c. 450–404 BC), well characterising the aristocratic Athenian statesman and general noted for his extravagant life-style and fine looks.*

V **Left** *Over-life-sized statues of two members of the court of Mausolus of Caria, made about 350 BC. Once set between the columns of the Mausoleum at Halicarnassus, they are often identified as Mausolus and Artemisia.*

VI **Above right** *Head cut from a bronze statue of Augustus found under the steps of a temple at Meroe (southern Sudan) and made about 27–25 BC.*

VII *A commemorative scabbard (above), found in Mainz, showing the ceding of military victory to Augustus by his stepson Tiberius, following a successful campaign in 16/15 BC. The coin (left), minted in Lyon in 15 BC, marks the same event.*

Antony's desertion of Octavian's sister Octavia for Cleopatra, Queen of Eygpt. Cleopatra posed a considerable threat to Octavian's position. Not only did she command extensive territory, great wealth and a large fleet, but she had borne Julius Caesar a son who, though illegitimate, could be considered to have a greater claim to Caesar's name and fortune than could Octavian.

In this period of growing tension Octavian's portrait changed. It could also have been the case that, eight years after Caesar's murder, the beard worn as a sign of mourning or vengeance was dated and losing appeal. Although Octavian presented himself as the Italian answer to the threat from the foreign queen of Egypt, he appeared in his new portraits as the successor to the kings who had ruled the eastern Mediterranean since the death of Alexander the Great. Indeed, this was where the battle for supremacy over Antony and Cleopatra was finally won by Octavian, in a naval engagement off the north-west coast of Greece near Actium in 31 BC.

What were the characteristics of Octavian's new look? His hair is windswept, his face animated, even agitated, suggesting tension and

44 *Veiled head from a marble statue of Octavian, made about 35–30 BC and found at La Alcudia (Majorca). Though shown here as a pious Roman citizen, a pose often adopted after 27 BC when Octavian became Augustus (fig. 46), the head is turned, the features contorted with apparent anxiety and the hair windswept in the manner of Hellenistic Greek royal portraits.*

energy. His head is turned to the right and looks up. There is much movement and, some suggest, emotion in portraits of this type, which draw upon Hellenistic Greek royal images and endow them with a sense of contemporary political turmoil.

Though related to the more dramatic portraits of the late Republic, the regal portraits of Octavian were unsuited to the image of a ruler who, having vanquished Antony and Cleopatra, claimed to restore the Roman Republic as a political system. In 28 and 27 BC Octavian formulated a new constitution in which this claim was made alongside the more justifiable view that he had saved the people of Rome from the anarchy of thirteen years of civil war. Octavian took the name Augustus offered to him by the Senate. Now he needed to present himself as no more than the first citizen of his own restored Republic. Clearly the earlier portrait, derived from traditions of royal portraiture in the Greek east, would not serve. Augustus also rejected the traditional form of Roman portrait used in regal fashion by Caesar. Instead he opted for an image based upon the Polykleitan ideal. At the time when Polykleitos was writing, the accurate portrayal of an individual's features was not attempted in public commemorations – his achievement could be rewarded with a commemorative statue, but the form of the figure was idealised (p. 39). Drawn from classical Greek principles, Augustus' image slipped into comparative anonymity. His head was no longer turned to one side and up, but faced forward and looked purposeful and reassuring rather than tense and energetic. The agitated hair was frozen in its tracks. The emperor's small, scarred body assumed heroic and perfect proportions. [46]

The date of the new portrait type is assured by its appearance on a coin [45] issued at the Asian city of Pergamon about 25 BC. Augustus' new image was shipped around the Empire. Over 250 portraits, almost all of them full-height statues, which is in itself an indication of the tendency to idealise, have survived. The number set up in antiquity must have been colossal: Augustus himself claimed that he had destroyed eighty silver statues in Rome alone, considering silver inappropriate for images of a mortal. Unusually for this period, there is no surviving record of any secretariat organising the despatch of imperial images. Nine out of ten were based upon the portrait created soon after the settlement of 27 BC, of which the Meroe head is surely an early example, combining the new [VI] three-lock fringe of hair with the Hellenistic Greek notion of the

45 *A silver cistophorus (below), a coin minted in Asia about 25 BC, compared with a glass intaglio portrait (bottom) of Augustus. The image on the coin dates the mature version of Augustus' portraits to the period following the constitutional settlement of 27 BC.*

46 *Statue of the emperor Augustus (27 BC – AD 14), shown as a pious Roman citizen veiled with the* sinus *(fold) of his toga; found in the Via Labicana, Rome. The static appearance of this figure contrasts with that of the veiled head of Octavian (fig. 44).*

strongly turned head. In general, the copies of Augustus' portrait are so alike that they must have been taken from plaster casts. Some provincial copyists, however, had scant idea of the original and misjudged the proportions. The image survived with little variation until Augustus' death in AD 14. Subsequently, when Augustus too was declared a god, the image was softened to suggest a benign and ever-youthful spirit still concerned for the welfare of the descendants of his subjects on earth.

As few of his subjects actually saw Augustus and most knew him from his image on coins and in statues, it is apparent that a certain control was exercised over those portraits destined for a wide audience. Augustus often appeared as the epitome of a pious Roman, his head veiled with the   46 *sinus* (shoulder-fold) of his toga. He might otherwise be shown as a general, though he never personally led troops into battle. Only on some coins (and certainly also in some statues which have not survived) of the period following Actium was the supreme nature of his power suggested. Signs of personal supremacy (such as the laurel wreath, a traditional Roman symbol of military victory, never the royal diadem) were otherwise slow to appear.

In the case of objects made for a very limited group of people whose loyalty was beyond question, however, Augustus apparently allowed the republican façade to drop. On cameos, probably made as gifts for senior officials and for members of the court, and on armour presented to the most senior ranks in the army, Augustus was portrayed as god-like supreme ruler. Thus in the scene on the mouthplate of a tinned bronze scabbard found in Mainz (Germany), Augustus, seated on a throne,   VII receives a statuette of Victory from an army commander, most likely his stepson Tiberius. Mars Ultor, the god of justifiable war and a personal patron of Augustus, stands in the background between the two figures, gazing at the emperor. Behind the throne a figure of Victory alights bearing a shield inscribed VIC[TORIA] AUG[USTI] (the victory of Augustus). Depicted here is the moment of transformation of military victory, won by Tiberius and his brother Drusus in Alpine campaigns against the Vindelici in 16–15 BC, into the victory of the emperor as head of state. In return for the shield offered him by Victory, and the statuette of Victory offered him by Tiberius, Augustus will give his stepson the shield leaning against his throne, inscribed FELICITAS TIBERI, a reference to Tiberius' valour and success in the field. In this scene, Augustus is portrayed half-naked and turned on his throne, a pose more readily associated with the god Jupiter. On coins such poses were not used until after Augustus' death, when he too was declared a god.

(left) A record of the same moment appears on contemporary coinage. In contrast to the scene on the scabbard, Augustus is shown trussed in drapery, and seated on a magistrate's folding stool set on a podium. Tiberius, who appears on some coins with Drusus, advances towards the emperor, offering a laurel branch in the same act of concession of military triumph. This modest ceremony is surely the version designed for public consumption.

Portraiture reflects a problem that obsessed Augustus throughout his long reign. It is evident from Suetonius' description that the emperor was not blessed with a strong constitution, and the succession troubled him from the start. Augustus' mausoleum was completed in the Campus Martius at Rome as early as 28 BC, an imperial tomb intended to house an imperial dynasty, despite the claims made at the time that Octavian (as he then was) intended to restore the Republic.

47 *Reverse of a silver denarius of Augustus, showing Gaius and Lucius Caesar with the spears and shields given them as* principes iuventutis *(leaders of Roman youth) by the Roman knights.*

Augustus had no son, and forced his daughter Julia into marriages more reflective of his interests than her own. In 21 BC she married Augustus' close friend and colleague Marcus Agrippa and bore him two sons, Gaius and Lucius. These were adopted as his own sons by Augustus, who taught them to read and to swim and to imitate his own handwriting. They accompanied him everywhere. They were granted public office at a precocious age, and Augustus himself resumed the consulship, the highest public office, after an interval of twenty years, in order to preside over their entry into public life.

Portraits of princes of the imperial family were used to familiarise people, especially the army, with the various candidates for the succession. Gaius and Lucius seem to have received maximum exposure. More portraits and dedications are known of them than of any other member of the imperial family save Augustus himself. In 5 and 2 BC they were made *principes iuventutis* (leaders of Roman youth) by the *equites*, the Roman knights, a powerful group of men of property. Dedications to them under this title were made all over the Empire, and 47 they appeared in this guise on the imperial coinage, bearing the spears and shields of their office. Augustus himself may have been responsible for the form of their portraits, in which they were presented as the new

Octavian and the new Augustus, a move that has caused no little confusion to modern scholars concerned with the identification of portraits of the princes and of the emperor. Unfortunately both princes died young, and Augustus was eventually obliged to accept as his successor his stepson Tiberius, the child of his wife Livia by an earlier marriage. Tiberius was forty-six when he was adopted; portraits commemorating the event suggest that he had found the elixir of youth. Augustus and Livia, too, never revealed their ages in their portraits: a group of busts from the Fayum (Egypt), made to commemorate Tiberius' adoption when the emperor and his consort were in their sixties, suggest vibrant youth and energy. A similar lack of interest in maturity is revealed in imperial coin portraits, in great contrast to republican practice. Indeed, the images of junior members of the imperial family are so bland that it is difficult to identify individuals without an accompanying inscription.

48

The importance of the family as the means of succession and in a more general sense as insurance for future stability was reflected in Augustan

48 *Marble bust of Tiberius Caesar. This portrait of Tiberius was devised to celebrate his adoption of Augustus' successor in* AD 4 *and deliberately shows him as younger than his age (46).*

social legislation, in which attempts were made to curb the divorce rate and to penalise the unmarried or childless. Portraits appeared showing members of the imperial family in nuclear groups: these vary in scale from a series of glass plaques issued to military officers to the grand figures on the Altar of Augustan Peace, a monument in the Campus Martius of Rome on which members of the imperial family and leading members of Roman society appeared incongruously in their private role as heads of families. Children are shown here for the first time on a major Roman public monument, tugging on togas and hushed by nurses. This is a striking departure from republican practice, in which no means was apparently evolved to portray the young, even those who died before their time.

Portraiture thus played a critical role in the establishment of the public identity of the first imperial family of Rome. A confusing picture survives in which it is difficult to distinguish portraits subject to imperial control from those made on the initiative of fearful subjects anxious to appease their new ruler. However, there can be little doubt that both agencies were prominent in the radical transformation of the role of portraiture from the exemplary masks of the Republic to the submissive imitations of the Empire.

49 *Glass medallion from Colchester of
about* AD 23, *showing Germanicus
Caesar with his children Nero,
Drusus III and Gaius (Caligula).*

CHAPTER 7

The Roman Image

The modern perception of the Roman image is one of austerity, of realism in a Cromwellian 'warts and all' fashion, and of an excessive devotion to the old and forbidding. It is well exemplified in the hundreds of funerary reliefs that have survived from late republican and early imperial Rome and from other settlements in Italy. These commemorative panels were originally set in the façades of specially constructed tombs, so that those portrayed within the frame appeared to stare at passers-by as if from a window, with the guarded air of expecting to confront a stranger. Though not particularly friendly in appearance, the subjects of Roman funerary reliefs do not menace. Indeed, their portraits exemplify unpretentious and unassuming behaviour. The subjects face forward, while those that are of a size to be dressed are modestly wrapped in cloaks, their hair cropped or strained back in unflattering style. However, if attention is paid to the inscriptions below the portraits, simple texts placed with care to identify

50, 57

50 *Lucius Ampudius Philomusus, freedman of Lucius and of an unnamed woman, portrayed with his wife (right) and daughter (left). This marble relief, originally set in the wall of the family tomb, was found near the Porta Capena, Rome, and made about 15–5 BC. The* modii *(corn measures) incised on either side of the portraits indicate that Philomusus was active in the corn trade.*

individual figures within each group, it becomes clear that many of the
names are very fanciful – Philomusus, for example, 'friend of the Muses'.
Such a name does not appear Roman at all, and raises the questions of
whom the reliefs portray and why the subjects of such portraits should
proclaim a Roman identity when their names suggest that they are
Greek.

50   The subjects of this particular family portrait are a freedman or former
slave and his wife and daughter. Their memorial is typical of much
Roman funerary art in that it tells the viewer quite a lot about the
subjects' social status and occupation in life, but nothing at all about
their religious beliefs or their feelings about death. On either side of the
portraits is a *modius*, a container used for storing corn, which states
pictorially that Philomusus was engaged in the corn trade. It is typical of
Roman convention that there should be no mention of his occupation in
the main text, which states that Philomusus was the former slave of
Lucius and of an unknown woman, conventionally indicated in the text
by a reversed C. On receiving his freedom, Philomusus became eligible
for Roman citizenship. He therefore has the Roman *tria nomina* (three
names), the first two of which were taken from his master Lucius
Ampudius, while he retained his slave name Philomusus as the third.
The name Philomusus does not necessarily imply ethnic Greek origin; it
was simply fashionable to have a Greek slave, and so a Roman might give
his slave a Greek name, even if he hailed from the wilder reaches of the
Danube. With his freedom Philomusus acquired the right to contract a
legal marriage, and for his family to become legitimate Roman citizens.
That is why his wife and daughter appear with him on the relief – at
least, we assume this to be the identity of the female figures, who are not
named in the text. Over 250 reliefs of this type have survived, of which
about eighty-five per cent were made at Rome in the reign of Augustus
(27 BC–AD 14), who passed laws improving the prospects of social
mobility for former slaves of non-Roman origin. The newly acquired
Roman identity of this family is proclaimed in the text below the
portraits, and in their modest dress, severe countenances and hairstyles.

These hairstyles are worthy of further inspection. Philomusus looks
like a Roman patrician, with shaven head, while his wife, to the right,
51   copies the coiffure of Livia, wife of the first emperor Augustus, as she
appeared towards the beginning of his long reign. Livia later changed

51 *Head from a marble
statue of Augustus' empress
Livia, showing the hairstyle
adopted in the early years
of his reign; made about
25–1 BC.*

her hairstyle, abandoning the distinctive Roman *nodus* or knot of hair above the brow in favour of a style more redolent of classical Greece. It is this later fashion that has been picked up by Philomusus' daughter.

The adoption of court fashions by the aspiring poor was new at Rome; the fashion had probably caught on from recently conquered Ptolemaic Egypt, where a cult of the ruling family had been rigidly enforced for centuries. A portrait survives of a woman resembling Cleopatra VII. It is likely that the subjects of such portraits as this are imitators of Cleopatra rather than the queen herself, who would hardly be portrayed without royal insignia such as the diadem. Nonetheless, her imitators copied not only Cleopatra's Greek hairstyle, but even her distinctive hooked nose. The imitation of the famous is not unknown today, though it has become in recent years an expression of flattery rather than of the stronger sentiments behind ancient practice: religious devotion, fear or appeasement.

In the age of Augustus, it was mainly younger men who aped court fashions; older males tended to look like republican Romans of the senatorial class. The point is well illustrated by a relief portraying two male freedmen, one young and the other old. Again, they sport a combination of Roman and Greek names, and the tools of their trades are

52

53

53 *Marble relief, made at Rome about 30–10 BC, of two freedmen flanked by the rods and axes (left) used in the ceremony of freeing a slave, and by the tools of a carpenter and a smith (right and above). The older man Publius Licinius Demetrius (right) has adopted a style of portrait formerly used by the Roman senatorial aristocracy; the younger man Publius Licinius Philonicus follows contemporary court fashions.*

illustrated around the margins of the relief along with the rods and staffs used in the ceremony of freeing a slave. Both portraits take the form of busts, in the fashion of the day rendered no further than the collar-bone, and without a trace of clothing. The younger man, Philonicus, has copied a hairstyle fashionable at the court of Augustus, while the older, Demetrius, has chosen to look like a Roman of the republican era, when commemorative portraiture was restricted by law to a small group of noble families and to the families of serving magistrates, most of whom belonged to the nobility.

The Romans of the Republic had well-established codes of practice concerning the nature and role of portraiture. Their peculiar customs attracted the interest of the Greek historian Polybius, who enjoyed a comfortable exile at Rome in the second century BC, well over a century before the Augustan freedmen's portraits were made. He observes (*Histories*, VI, 53):

> When a Roman nobleman dies, he is carried, upright wherever possible, into the Forum to the so-called *rostra*. An adult son or, in his absence, some other suitable relative, ascends the *rostra* to speak on the virtues and

achievements of the dead man. The loss affects the crowd, not just the principal mourners. After the interment they place an image of the deceased in the most conspicuous part of the house, inside a wooden shrine. This image is a mask, reproducing with remarkable fidelity the features and complexion of the deceased. These images are displayed at public sacrifices, when they are decorated with much care. When any distinguished member of the family dies, the images are taken to the funeral, the masks worn by men who bear the closest resemblance to the original in stature and bearing. These representatives wear togas, with a purple border if the deceased were a consul or praetor, whole purple if he had been a censor, and embroidered with gold if he had celebrated a triumph. All the representatives of the dead ride in chariots preceded by the *fasces* [rods of office], axes and other insignia appropriate to the office held by the deceased in life, and when they reach the *rostra* they sit on a row of ivory chairs. There could not be a more ennobling sight for a young man who aspires to fame and virtue. For who would not be inspired by the sight of images of men renowned for their excellence, all portrayed together as if they were alive and breathing? What spectacle could be more glorious than this?

Polybius' eyewitness account was amplified by the encyclopaedist Pliny the Elder, writing in the mid-first century AD when the custom had still been practised within living memory. Pliny observes with disapproval the contemporary fashion of covering the walls of old houses with old master paintings and portraits of 'strangers', perhaps a reference to the practice, well documented archaeologically, of keeping portraits of Greek men of culture and even of Hellenistic Greek rulers in Roman villas. He complains (*Natural History*, XXXV, 2–5):

As for themselves, they're only interested in portraying personal wealth, and, since their minds are not portrayed, bodily features are also neglected. It was not so in the *atria* [halls] of our ancestors: portraits were displayed for admiration, not statues by foreign artists, nor bronzes or marbles, but wax models of faces, each set out on a separate sideboard, to provide likenesses to be carried at the funerals of members of the family group, and always when a member of the family died the entire company of that house that had ever formed part of it was present. The family trees were also traced by lines set near the portraits. The domestic archives were filled with records and written memorials of public careers. Outside the house and around the doorways there were other images of those mighty characters, with captured spoils of war fastened to them. Even if the house were sold, these were not removed, but served as an incentive to less warlike owners.

The written accounts of Polybius and Pliny provide precious evidence for the role and the form of early Roman portraits, which appear so different from the Greek. At Rome, portraits were a privilege enjoyed by the few. Images of ancestors were used to instil traditional virtues in the young, by the effective method of role-play at ceremonies that would in themselves arouse much emotion. Family life was literally lived in the presence of ancestors, whose images were displayed in those parts of the house most frequented by guests and others dependent upon the patronage of the head of the household. Great men and women were never forgotten, and it is clear from Pliny's account that families were not above claiming a few extra if the supply were felt to be deficient. Outside the house, the *gens*, or extended family group, was further strengthened by the public display of ancestral portraits at funerals. The portraits themselves celebrated the traditional Roman virtues of respect for austerity, authority and for the old. Because they were taken from death-masks, the images replicated exactly the features of advanced age and of appearance at death: folded, wrinkled skin, replete with blemishes; shaven head; the mouth turned down.

From the sculptor's point of view, the starting point for a republican portrait was surely very different from that for a contemporary Hellenistic Greek. As Roger Hinks put it (*Carolingian Art*, 1935, p. 123f.):

> The Hellenistic portrait was the ideal reconstruction of a personality, in which accidental facts of nature were indeed accepted and used, though only as the starting point for an imaginative exercise in concretised psychology. The Roman portraitist, on the other hand, approached his sitter objectively, not subjectively; he looked from the outside at the features one by one and transliterated them piecemeal into the language of art. The resulting work was both a document and a commentary, but the former aspect was more clearly defined than the latter. The Roman portrait was the exact statement of a particular case; it was as far removed as possible from the generalised and the typical.

The latter part of Hinks' account offers a good description of 'verism', as the apparently realistic style of Roman portraiture is called. It is very difficult, though, to distinguish the documentary element in portraits of those who, like the freedmen's families, were simply trying to look like Romans. Moreover, no wax masks have survived, nor are there portraits of Romans in more durable materials that may be securely dated to the time of Polybius, the mid-second century BC. In the succeeding century, however, the demand for commemorative portraits grew with the intense struggle for individual leadership that signalled the end of the Republic. Although elements of old usage were retained into the early Empire, portraiture came to be used in a more public and competitive way. For the Romans, the long-established association of portraits with death-masks meant that the head remained the crucial element, and the head therefore retained for a long time some link with verism, however idealised or romanticised the body. In this respect it is instructive to compare a mid-first-century head, apparently copied from a death-mask, with a marble portrait bust dating from the later years of that century, 54 which evidently represents a live subject, but retains qualities of ancestral portraiture. Some examples survive from the first century BC of Roman heads carved in the veristic tradition and set on bodies of heroised 55

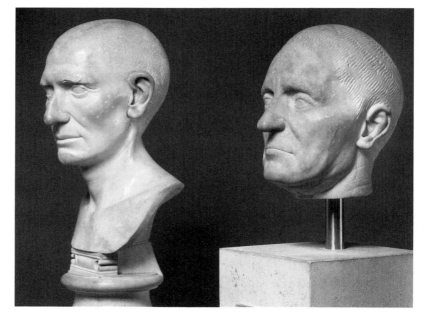

54 *Marble heads of two Romans with shaven heads, the portrait on the left apparently taken from life and made about* 30–1 BC, *and the one on the right apparently based on a death mask and made about* 60–40 BC.

Hellenistic Greek form. Odd hybrids to the modern eye, these reflect the Roman conquest of Greek lands, and the consequent adoption by individual Romans, notably military officers, of almost regal images in the increasingly competitive and unsettled society of the late Republic, a time in which political leaders acquired private armies and individual Romans appointed kings, even if they themselves spurned a royal diadem. In contrast to the militaristic contemporary climate, late republican writers give the impression that early republican commemorative portraiture was largely civic in nature: statues of early republican heroes and even heroines were dressed in togas, not armour.

In the first half of the first century BC, ancestral portraits began to appear on coins minted by young magistrates, the *tresviri monetales*, who were annually appointed to a board with the right to advertise themselves on their products. This they did in the traditional fashion, not with portraits of themselves but with images of distinguished ancestors. Some, significantly, even counted kings of appropriately similar name amongst their progenitors – Titus Vettius Sabinus, for example, showed the legendary early king Tatius; Lucius Marcius Philippus showed Ancus Marcius. Marcus Claudius Marcellus, consul in 222 BC and five times in all, appeared on a coin of his descendant Marcellinus minted in the mid-first century BC. Gaius Antius Restio, tribune of the plebs in 72 BC, appears on a coin minted by his descendant a quarter of a century later. Some of these portraits would not be out of place as images of contemporary figures, and it is widely held that their style reflects current fashions rather than those of the times of the kings or of Marcellus.

The first Roman to be commemorated in his lifetime on coins was Julius Caesar, *dictator* at Rome from 48 to 44 BC. Although Caesar looked like a republican nobleman in his portraits, his use of portraiture

55 *Marble statue of a Roman military officer; from Chieti, central Italy, and made about 70–40 BC. His body is shown in heroic Greek fashion, but the head is evidently in the Roman veristic style.*

56 *Portraits of (a) Gaius Antius Restio on a coin of his descendant minted in 47 BC, (b) the legendary king Tatius on a coin of Titus Vettius Sabinus minted in 70 BC and (c) Julius Ceasar on a coin minted in Rome shortly before his assassination in March 44 BC.*

a
b
c

departed from republican norms. Not only did he break the taboo on contemporary portraits by appearing in his lifetime on his coinage, but he even permitted his statues, of which there were many, to be carried on litters as if they were images of a god, and allowed them to be set next to images of deities on sacred platforms. This was highly controversial, and created a problem for Caesar's heir Octavian (later Augustus).

For his own portraits, Augustus developed a style derived from the ideal representation of human form developed in classical Greece. As we have seen, the 'warts and all' Roman portrait, formerly reserved for the republican aristocracy, had become by the reign of Augustus the *déclassé* sign of the rising older freedman, but it also continued in use for those free-born Romans who had not adopted the classicising fashions of Augustus' court. Thus in a grand version of the freedman relief, Antistius Sarculo, a free-born Roman and a member of the Salian order of priests who were charged with the ceremonies attending the opening and closure of the military campaign season, is portrayed in traditional guise. The relief is of particular interest for the double portrait of Sarculo with his wife Antistia Plutia, one of his former slaves. From the portraits alone it is impossible to judge the gulf in social origin that lay between the pair, though the facts are stated baldly enough in the accompanying text.

Augustus did much else to change the landscape of portraiture at Rome. In the Republic, public statues had been erected of magistrates

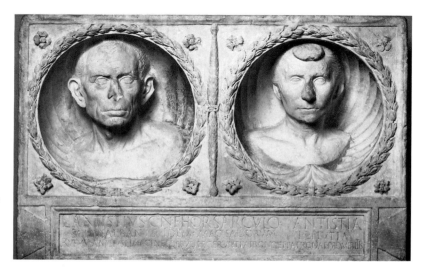

57 *Marble relief commemorating the free-born Lucius Antistius Sarculo and his wife and former slave Antistia Plutia; from Rome, where it was made about 30–10 BC. The monument was set up by former slaves of the family, and the gulf in social origin of husband and wife finds no expression in the portraits.*

who had reached at least the rank of aedile. Though the Capitol at Rome was reserved for national heroes, the Roman Forum was so choked with statues as to have been subject to clearance by the censors at various times in the second century BC. Under Augustus, the Capitol and the Forum became reserved for images of members of the imperial house. Another new feature of imposing dimensions was Augustus' Forum, his own ancestral gallery, which denied the recent experience of thirteen years of civil war by presenting the first emperor as the natural successor to Romulus and Aeneas. Honours for serving magistrates were no longer in the gift of the Senate, but depended on the relationship of individual officers with the emperor. The nobles could still keep ancestral portraits at home and bring them out for funerals in the fashion of the Republic, but even this was subject to political constraint; the family of the conspirator Piso, for example, who was accused of intrigue against Augustus' overwhelmingly popular step-grandson Germanicus Caesar, were not permitted to parade Piso's image at funerals, and the ban was ratified in a decree of the Senate preserved in a copy inscribed on bronze tablets recently discovered in Spain.

Under the Empire, ancestral portraiture thus came to assume a more limited and private function. The exemplary role of republican portraiture was gradually lost, and, deprived of a mass audience at funerals and festivals, the genre gradually withered away. From the reign of Augustus onwards, the living emperor and his court, rather than ancestors, served as models for his subjects, many of whom copied court hairstyles and even imperial physiognomies. The new role of non-imperial portraiture was to express the relationship of citizen to emperor or, as Pliny justifiably complained, to commemorate the material success of individuals within contemporary society, as there no longer existed any interest in martial prowess or moral excellence.

Though the function of the traditional Roman portrait disappeared, the form of the image survived. It did not long remain the preserve of freed slaves: once these had become absorbed within Roman society as a result of Augustan social legislation, freedmen reliefs ceased to be made, and their subjects adopted the motifs of decorative imperial art to adorn their tombs. However, the traditional 'warts and all' style of portrait remained a means of expressing Roman identity, and thus passed from the city of Rome through Italy to those areas conquered by the Romans which competed with each other for privileged status within the Empire. For example, funerary altars very like the freedmen reliefs in style appear in the Greek-speaking provinces about a century later. There is no local input to this style of portrait beyond the Greek inscription identifying the subjects. In north Africa, bust-length portraits of the deceased were made in Cyrenaica (Libya) for the first time in the first century AD. Here and in neighbouring Egypt the portraits took on local forms. In Cyrenaica, miniature bust-length portraits were carved in imported marble and were set in cuttings in the walled courts of rock-cut tombs. In Egypt, some portraits were carved in wood to form coffin lids; these were set vertically within the tomb and provided with wooden flaps which could be opened to reveal the head and bust of the deceased, rather as the Roman freedmen's portraits had appeared to gaze from a window. Particularly evocative are the bust-length portraits painted in encaustic or tempera on wood and set into the wraps of a mummy, over the head of the deceased.

In all these regions, the notion of providing a bust of the deceased as he or she had appeared in life was a Roman introduction, as were the less universally applied ideas of carving the busts in relief, naming the individuals portrayed and setting the portrait to confront the viewer as if from a window. The traditional portrait of the Roman Republic, shorn of its associations with the exclusive patrician nobility, thus became the sign of Roman identity most closely linked with the humbler but aspiring classes of provincial imperial society. However, the Roman image was not condemned to permanent exile on distant imperial frontiers: it reappeared in Rome at the courts of emperors who were themselves of relatively modest origin, or who had some political interest in reasserting traditional values, such as Vespasian in the later first century and the short-lived soldier emperors of the third century AD. In this context the Roman image was recycled yet again, as the wealthier provincials dutifully imitated their ruler's hairstyle and physical characteristics.

58 *Marble relief portrait of a woman with crimped hair. Designed to fit into a niche in the courtyard of a tomb, this type of portrait and its setting are Roman innovations within the funerary art of Cyrenaica. The hairstyle was current in Rome about AD 160–180.*

CHAPTER 8

Bearded and Beardless Men

The fashion for growing or shaving a beard shifted throughout classical Greek and Roman antiquity, and was more than a question of personal taste or of following a particular mode: to be bearded or shaven was then a sign of age, of moral values or even of ethnic identity.

A beard is a matter of immediate visual import, and even today forms an early point of departure for the kind of description of individuals devised by officials in, say, police or immigration departments. In modern times, the wearing of a beard and long hair has sometimes signified disaffection from a political regime, or individual rebellion against conservative social norms. Some twentieth-century regimes have found beards so threatening as to ban them altogether, shaving bearded foreigners at the frontier. This was the case in Greece under the colonels in the late 1960s and early 1970s.

The irony of the Greek *junta*'s ban on beards was not lost on classical scholars, who were well aware that the growth of a beard in archaic and classical Greece signified maturity and wisdom. A clean-shaven face was associated with youthful beauty and often with dissolute behaviour: many examples survive, notably on painted vases and in Roman copies of portraits of well-known individuals such as Alcibiades. Greek fashions were followed by some sectors of Etruscan society. Beards and long hair also served as signs of mature wisdom in early Rome (Varro, *De re rustica*, II, XI, 10). Varro relates that the first barbers to arrive in Rome from Sicily set up shop in 300 BC. A monument to their introduction by the patron Publius Titinius Mena was erected at Ardea, near Rome, where it could still be admired in Varro's day (the first century BC). The supposed date of the barbers' arrival coincides neatly with the establishment by his successors of the cult of Alexander of Macedon. The designs on contemporary coins indicate that Rome and the Greek cities of southern Italy

IV

56b

were quick to adopt the clean-shaven features of Alexander's portrait for representations of formerly bearded heroes such as Hercules, but no undisputed Roman portraits of this period survive, and the coincidence with the introduction of shaving at Rome may be fortuitous.

Although Alexander's looks were imitated by many of his successors in the Hellenistic kingdoms of the eastern Mediterranean, portraits surviving from the Greek communities which then came under Macedonian rule include images of bearded philosophers, poets and orators; moreover, the evidence of funerary sculpture shows that beards were also worn by Greeks of mature years but no particular cultural distinction.

A good example of the 'city-father' portrait is that of Herodes Atticus, the millionaire Athenian philosopher who tutored the future emperors Marcus Aurelius and Lucius Verus. Herodes' portrait may be securely identified by matching his features against an inscribed portrait that has survived from Corinth. Although he had a professional interest in looking like a Greek philosopher, and evidently dressed for the part, Herodes also completed a full Roman career (*cursus honorum*), culminating in the consulship. Yet there is nothing Roman about Herodes' portrait, which may be explained as a local Greek development so archaising in appearance that it has been confused with late classical funerary art.

59 *Marble portrait head of the millionaire philosopher and politician Tiberius Claudius Atticus Herodes (AD 101–177), Roman consul and a controversial figure in the civic life of Athens, his native city. Though Herodes reached the highest position in Roman public life, his portrait lacks any reference to contemporary Rome and has been confused with classical Greek funerary portraits.*

The 'Alexander look' was eventually picked up by some Roman generals who campaigned in the eastern Mediterranean in the first century BC, when Alexander had become a distant, though evidently still powerful, memory. Pompey, like Alexander called Magnus (the Great), was the foremost Roman imitator of Alexander – appropriately enough, for Pompey appointed kings and created new provinces of the growing empire, and certainly held more power than had any Roman before him.

Private portraits of members of leading republican families and of magistrates evolved from very different ancestral traditions. There is no surviving evidence for influence from the Hellenistic Greek world upon the development of portraiture at Rome before the late Republic, and even then the Roman tradition of 'verism' remained of critical importance to the portrayal of heads.

Surviving portraits of men of the Roman Republic, engraved on gems or cameos or sculptured in relief or in the round, and almost all of the first century BC, reveal lean, beardless heads with closely cropped or shaven hair, austere features and a marked tendency to record warts, wrinkles and other physical imperfections. However, although they look very different from classical Greek portraits, Roman republican portraits expressed regard for a very similar set of virtues to those commemorated in Greek images of distinguished statesmen and men of letters, namely a respect for old age, austerity, wisdom and authority. Both clean-shaven Roman republican and bearded classical Greek portraits explicitly rejected the idealisation of youth, physical perfection and, above all, the ambiguous status, half mortal and half divine, conveyed in the portraiture of Alexander and his successors.

The austere Roman version of the shaven look, modified by the classicising portraits of the first emperor Augustus, lasted into the second century AD. Beards were worn at Rome by young adults and were then ritually removed and dedicated to the gods in a ceremony celebrated at the age of twenty-four. This is recorded by many authors, including the satirist Juvenal (3, 186), the biographer Suetonius (*Caligula*, 10; *Nero*, 12) and the historian Dio Cassius (XLVIII, 34, 3; LXI, 19, 1; LXXIX, 14, 4). Until the time of Hadrian, we are told, the emperors followed this ancient practice (Dio Cassius, LXVIII, 15, 5). The same author notes (XLVIII, 34, 3) that Octavian shaved off his beard at twenty-four, 'just

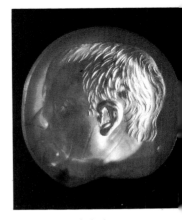

60 *Engraved chalcedony portrait of a middle-aged Roman, perhaps a senior military officer or politician, with close-cropped hair and a wart on his chin. Perhaps used as a personal seal or worn as a sign of allegiance, and made about 75–50 BC.*

like the rest'. Behind this act, it was insinuated, lay an adulterous passion for his future consort Livia, whom he no doubt wished to impress with his maturity. The evidence of the coin portraits tells another, more public, story: the bearded portraits lasted another three years, perhaps as a sign of mourning or vengeance for the murder of Octavian's adoptive father Julius Caesar. 43a

Some Romans continued to wear a beard into adult life: the reliefs of the Column of Trajan in Rome or the Arch of Trajan erected at Beneventum suggest it was at least a convenience for campaigning soldiers. However, in late republican and early imperial Rome, beards mainly signified, in a startling reversal of Greek practice, relative immaturity, the act of mourning or the marking of disaster. Literary figures took a more positive view: Cicero implies (*Pro Caelio*, 33) that youths with downy beards were favoured by Roman matrons – the mark, perhaps, of the late republican toy-boy. Moreover, at Rome, as in Hellenistic Greece, a mature beard could signify a personal commitment to Greek culture. In this context we find isolated examples of mature eminent bearded Romans in the centuries before such a commitment became universally acceptable at the court of the emperor Hadrian.

These incidents are bound up with the Roman conquest of Greece, and reflect the attitude of powerful Roman individuals towards Greek culture. The earliest concerns Titus Quinctius Flamininus, consul in 198 BC, who celebrated a victory over Philip V of Macedon at Cynocephalae in 197 BC, thereby freeing the Greeks from Macedonian rule but advancing the cause of Roman domination. It was the former result that was stressed in subsequent celebrations, and marked in the issue of a series of gold staters bearing Flamininus' name and portrait. He is shown in the manner of Macedonian kings, with long fly-away hair and a moderately heavy beard. The portrait is so close to that of Flamininus' defeated enemy Philip that it is thought to be a product of the same atelier. The image may then be explained as a portrait of a Roman ruler made in the Greek manner by local craftsmen, or, from the Roman point of view, as an example of a Roman adopting the image of his defeated enemy, thereby destroying and humiliating Philip's public identity. From either perspective this is the earliest portrait of a Roman in the Greek manner to have survived. It is not clear whether the large issue of gold coins, apparently the product of different dies, was made to commemorate Flamininus' victory or his proclamation of freedom for all the Greeks, made in the stadium at Isthmia (near Corinth) in 196 BC. The coins may have been intended, like later imperial cameos, as gifts to favoured individuals.

Two hundred and sixty-one years later, when Greece had long since become a province of the Roman Empire, its freedom from taxation and Roman interference in internal affairs was proclaimed – once more in the stadium at Isthmia – on this occasion by the emperor Nero (AD 54–68). A fanatical admirer of Greek culture, Nero, like Flamininus, was occasionally portrayed bearded. The emperor is also said to have inaugurated a new festival, appropriately called the Juvenalia, in which the hairs of his first beard were placed in a globe and offered to Jupiter Capitolinus. To celebrate this rite of passage to manhood, the nobility dutifully performed charades (Suetonius, *Nero*, 12).

The philhellene emperor Domitian (AD 81–96) also appeared bearded on some of his coins. By this time, a few stone portraits of bearded private individuals were being made. These may be distinguished from

61

61 *Marble bust of a young man with a short beard and tiers of waved hair. The angular planes of the face and the size and shape of the bust indicate that this is a rare bearded portrait of the later first century* AD.

portraits of bearded men of Hadrianic date – made before it became customary to engrave the eyes – by the shape of the beard, which in first-century portraits is short and trimmed square around the cheekbones, and by the planes of the face, more angular than in portraits of the second century and later. Some witty remarks about fashions in shaving also survive from this period, of which Martial's epigram will serve as an example: 'Part of your face is clipped, part is shaven. Part is plucked. Whoever would think it to be one head?' (VII, 95, 11).

The first appearance of bearded men in private portraiture of the Roman Empire is complemented by surviving literary accounts from the Greek-speaking provinces which reflect a growing awareness of Greek identity and an interest in traditional Greek culture. From the orator Dio of Prusa and the philosopher Apollonius of Tyana we learn that beards were regarded as the mark of the Hellene. In two letters of Apollonius, beards were specifically linked with the Greek mother-cities of Athens and Sparta, which were to play a great role in the revival of Hellenic culture in the second century AD.

Dio of Prusa in Bithynia (north-west Asia Minor), in a speech given before AD 97, (XXXVI, 17), praised the Borysthenic Greeks of the region of Olbia (Ukraine):

> A philosopher would have been hugely pleased to see them, as they were all of the old style, as Homer describes the Greeks, long-haired and with flowing beards, and only one of them was clean-shaven, and he was subjected to the ridicule and resentment of them all. They said that he shaved not from personal whim but to cultivate the Romans and show his friendship towards them. So anyone could see from his example the shameful nature of this habit and how unsuited it is to real men.

Apollonius, writing to the Lacedaemonians (Spartans), probably in the reign of Hadrian, disdains shaving as effeminate (*Epistles*, LXIII):

> I have set eyes on your beardless men, their thighs and legs smooth and white, wearing soft light tunics, their fingers and necks dripping with fine jewels, their feet shod in Ionic style. I did not therefore recognise your envoys, though your letter spoke of them as Lacedaemonians.

In another letter to the Saites of Egypt, probably contemporary with the above, Apollonius mocks the Athenians (*Epistles*, LXX):

How they have ceased to be Hellenes, I shall explain. No wise old man is an Athenian, for no Athenian ever grew a full beard, since no one ever grew a beard at all.

A third letter of Apollonius to the Ionian Greeks does not mention beards, but makes it clear that appearance and nomenclature were regarded as signs of ethnic identity (*Epistles*, LXXI):

You think that you should be called Hellenes because of your pedigree and because you were once [Greek] colonies, but, just as the Hellenes are known by their customs, laws, language and lifestyle, so are men known by their external form and appearance. But most of you have even abandoned your names, and on account of your recent prosperity you have forfeited all the symbols of your ancestors. So it is quite right that they no longer make you welcome at their tombs, for they no longer recognise you. For those who were formerly named after heroes, sea-captains and legislators are now called Lucullus and Fabricius and other blessed Lucanian names.

62 *Portrait in relief of a man and his wife, early second century* AD. *Though the inscription below is in Greek and the relief is believed to come from Smyrna (Asia Minor), the images reflect the increasingly Romanised appearance of the Greek people, so lamented by Dio of Prusa (compare with figs 50, 53, 57).*

The inference is clear enough: by profiting from the Roman imperial peace, by gaining Roman citizenship and adopting Roman names, and finally by imitating the Romans in appearance, the Greeks stood in danger of losing their identity. The criticisms made in these letters find some basis in surviving imperial correspondence and in archaeological remains, which attest the competitive prosperity of Greek communities of the period, notably of cities in Bithynia and Asia (northwest and western Asia Minor). On some funerary stelae from the same area, the subjects are portrayed frontally at bust-length in the manner of early Roman freedmen reliefs, the men with shaven faces, and both 62 sexes with hairstyles imitating current fashions at the Roman imperial 63, court.

Endorsement of the intellectuals' concern with Greek identity was to come from an unlikely source. In AD 113, four years before becoming emperor, Hadrian served as *archon* (chief magistrate) of the city of

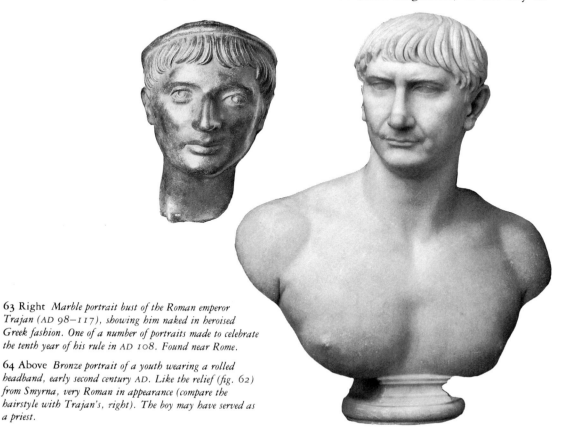

63 Right *Marble portrait bust of the Roman emperor Trajan (AD 98–117), showing him naked in heroised Greek fashion. One of a number of portraits made to celebrate the tenth year of his rule in AD 108. Found near Rome.*

64 Above *Bronze portrait of a youth wearing a rolled headband, early second century AD. Like the relief (fig. 62) from Smyrna, very Roman in appearance (compare the hairstyle with Trajan's, right). The boy may have served as a priest.*

Athens. After his accession, Athens was given unprecedented privileges and the status of the city was greatly enhanced by its position as head of the Panhellenion, the union of all cities of Greek origin founded by Hadrian himself in AD 131–2. Hadrian's personal commitment to Greek culture was reflected in many ways, not least in his personal appearance. Portraits of Hadrian before his accession are notoriously difficult to identify. As emperor, his beard, worn in the style of Pericles of Athens, was retained until his death, despite the jibes of his more conservative contemporaries against 'the little Greek', and those of his biographer that his beard was grown expressly to conceal unsightly blemishes on his skin (Scriptores Historiae Augustae, *Hadrian*, 26).

> O lovely whiskers, o inspirational mop!
> But if growing a beard, my friend, means acquiring wisdom,
> Any old goat can be Plato.
>
> Lucian of Samosata, *Meditation on Bearers*, XI, 430

65 *Marble bust of the emperor Hadrian (AD 117–138), shown in military dress; found in Hadrian's villa at Tivoli, near Rome. Compare the beard and the serene features with those of the classical Greek statesman Pericles (fig. 1), also in military dress.*

66 Above *Over-life-sized marble bust of the emperor Antoninus Pius (AD 138–161), shown in military dress; found in the house of Jason Magnus, a local notable, at Cyrene (eastern Libya). Pius continued the tradition of wearing a beard established by Hadrian.*

67 Above right *Over-life-sized marble bust of the emperor Marcus Aurelius (AD 161–180); from the same site as fig. 66. Marcus wore a longer beard indicative of his personal commitment to philosophy.*

With Hadrian we enter the age of the bearded man. Henceforth virtually all mature Romans were portrayed bearded, a dramatic reversal of the earlier practice in which beards had been ritually discarded as a sign of immaturity. The first beard must still have been shaved, so there is no reason to suppose the end of the long-established rite of passage to manhood. However, the commemorative shaven portrait, still prevalent under Trajan, was abandoned in favour of an image with similar moral connotations but also expressive of Greek identity. By the mid-second century, the late classical 'city-father' and 'philosopher' portraits were revived and accepted at the highest levels of Roman society, and with them came an often passionate interest in classical culture. Nowhere was this more apparent than in Greece itself: outside the major cities and sanctuaries, modest funerary reliefs indicate the rapid spread of beards beyond the professional classes. Indeed, the fashion for beards spread throughout the Empire, and was evidently not restricted to Hellenophiles. No doubt this came of Hadrian's personal example, for his portraits were widely circulated on coins and many statues of him were dedicated in the provinces. The emperor himself was an unusually energetic traveller, who intervened considerably in provincial affairs.

Probably to emphasise continuity, Hadrian's adopted successor
66 Antoninus Pius (AD 138–61) was bearded, although he never visited
Greece as emperor and displayed little enthusiasm for Greek affairs.

Pius' successor Marcus Aurelius (AD 161–80) was the first Roman
67 emperor to adopt the long beard, the mark of the serious philosopher, in
a move that continued to be influential, even long after his death. The
short-lived emperor Macrinus (AD 217–18), for example, grew a long
beard in imitation of Marcus (Herodian, 5, 2, 3–4); the change from
68 short to long beard may be traced on his coinage.

The fashion for beards lasted until the revival, engineered by the
emperor Constantine (AD 306–37), of the Augustan version of the
traditional Roman clean-shaven image. In the interim, beards survived a
series of military coups and the rule of Empire by uncultured and ill-
8 shaven soldiers of humble Balkan origin. Though most men followed
imperial fashion, beards also survived the rise of Christianity as the
official religion of the Empire, and acquired, not for the first or last time,
an association with the intellectual and the political nonconformist.

68 *Coin of the emperor Macrinus (AD 217–218), who
grew a beard in deliberate imitation of Marcus Aurelius.*

CHAPTER 9

Dress

To the student of ancient portraiture, dress is never a casual reflection of transient fashion: its use – or the lack of it – is worthy of careful consideration. Hairstyles, much studied in portraiture of the Roman Empire for their dependence upon court fashion and hence for their value in dating portraits of private citizens, may also reflect the contemporary moral climate or suggest an interest in past cultures. Dress and hairstyle place the subject of a portrait within the prevailing social order, and it often happened in antiquity that this consideration was of greater importance to the patron than the portrayal of individual character.

Awareness of quality, style and suitability in dress goes back to remote antiquity. Archaic Greek sculptures and painted vases reflect an

69 *Detail of a* hydria *(water-jar), made in Athens about 440–430 BC. A woman, perhaps a nanny, dressed in a* peplos *with sleeves pushed up, hands an infant to his mother seated in a pose of authority, a wool-basket in front of her to emphasise her commitment to domestic life.*

evident concern with the pattern, weight and texture of clothes. Regional styles of dress were clearly distinguished, and became associated with ethnic identity and even with moral values.

The mother, the nurse, the servant, the mistress of the household and the *hetaira* (prostitute) are among the women represented on painted vases made in classical Athens; even today they may be identified in these roles by their dress and their pose. Indeed, they appear considerably more lifelike than the earliest surviving monumental portraits of individual women made in the mid-fourth century BC. The subjects of these stone portraits are women of the court of Mausolus of Caria, and they appear on his monumental tomb. Among the better-preserved heads is one often identified (with no good reason) as Mausolus' sister-queen Artemisia; a very similar representation of a woman identified as Ada, successor to Artemisia, was found in the temple of Athena Polias at Priene in western Asia Minor. By the time these images were made, portraits of famous men were well established, but for the female members of the Carian ruling family a portrait type had to be invented. The hairstyle shared by both women is quite distinctive but its source is uncertain. In Carian court portraiture, dress was less reflective of real life than we may suppose the representations on Greek vases to be; where the torsos survive, the women of Mausolus' court are dressed in sumptuous tunics and cloaks in the Greek style but arranged like the drapery on

70 *Marble portrait heads of women, 360–330 BC, from (left) the Mausoleum at Halicarnassus and (right) the Temple of Athena Polias at Priene, western Asia Minor. The women have similar hairstyles, with a sakkos (hood) behind the tiers of curls framing the full face. In appearance these women are less lifelike than the earlier genre representations of women on Athenian vases (fig. 69).*

statues of goddesses. Images of these powerful women rulers and of the queens of the Hellenistic kingdoms hardly conveyed an individual likeness; indeed, no distinctive physiognomy was to emerge among Hellenistic queens before the reign of Cleopatra VII of Egypt (d. 30 BC), by which time the rulers of the Greek east were struggling with the military leaders of the disintegrating Roman Republic for individual mastery of the Mediterranean world, and the style of contemporary portraits had come to be influenced by Roman verism.

41,

Portraits of Roman women were mostly more idealised than those of men, though there survive some splendid examples of female verism in which the Roman admiration for authority and austerity has been transferred lock, stock and barrel to women. Indeed, ancestral portraits of women were kept in cabinets in the houses of the nobility and paraded alongside those of famous men. Statues of heroines of the early Republic were displayed in early imperial Rome: Cloelia was even portrayed in a toga, which by the time of record had become a garment restricted to men. Most Roman women wore Greek dress – a sleeveless tunic with

71

71 *Marble portrait bust dedicated by a freed slave, Epithymetus, in memory of his patron Claudia Olympias, daughter of Tiberius. Described in the text as most dutiful (a quintessentially Roman virtue, see fig. 46), Claudia Olympias is portrayed as a stern middle-aged matron, though her austere features contrast with an elaborate tiered hairstyle and opulent dress.*

fastenings gathered on the shoulders (*chiton*) and a draped mantle. The Hellenistic royal notion of arranging the drapery in the manner of statues of deities was taken up for portraiture in the Roman Empire, both for members of the imperial family and for images of private citizens. Modesty was a recurrent theme: one of the most popular images, unhelpfully dubbed by scholars the 'large or small Herculanean woman' after the type was identified at the site of Herculaneum on the Bay of Naples, portrays the woman drawing her cloak to conceal her breasts, a gesture that makes the subject seem exclusive and unattainable, and, on a more practical level, forces the tunic out into v-shaped folds above the concealed cleavage, a feature noted even in minor portraits.

IX

Under the Empire, women, like men, copied imperial hairstyles and the idea of expressing Roman identity in their appearance. Beyond such behaviour, which we have already considered, hairstyles and dress are interesting indicators of moral tone. Thus the Augustan climate of moral restraint is well observed in female portraits of that emperor's reign (27 BC–AD 14). The hair was pulled back in a most unflattering style, and tightly coiled into plaits of a type to be seen again in societies attempting to impose a homespun simplicity upon a sophisticated population – Victorian England, for example, or Nazi Germany. As soon as the old emperor died, there seems to have been a palpable sense of release, again well expressed in women's hairstyles, which began to escape their bonds and tumble down the neck. In place of the strained forehead, there appear kiss-curls, built up into serried ranks above the brow. By the late first century, these had become towering edifices anticipating the fashions of eighteenth-century Europe. They must have been achieved

51

72a

71,
b&c,
II

72 *Cameos illustrating the changes in women's hairstyles from the first to the third century* AD: *a) portrait of the elder Agrippina, a long lock falling down the side of her neck and a* queue *at the nape, wearing the* stola *over her tunic, about* AD 37–41; *b) woman with a similar* queue *but with tiers of curls above the brow,* AD 60–80; *c) woman of African appearance with high tiers of curls and a* stola *over her tunic,* AD 90–100; *d) woman, perhaps Sabina, with plaits wrapped around her head, about* AD 110–130; *e) woman with a large coiled bun at the back of her head, about* AD 180; *f) woman with a flattened plait coiled at the back of her head, about* AD 200–230.

b c d e f

a

with wigs or hairpieces. Under Trajan there was a reaction, and the coquettish styles were confined into matronly tiers rising to an unflattering peak. Hadrian, as we might expect, encouraged a revival of Greek fashions in hairstyles. Under his successor, Pius, the elegant Hadrianic bun turned into a flattened plait which gradually slid to the back of the head, assuming ever larger proportions, and then in the third century AD started a new ascent, with the vogue for a most unattractive roll of hair taken up from the nape to the crown, where the ends were tucked under. Unaccountably (as it seems to the modern spectator) this style remained in fashion for much of later antiquity. What we see in such portraits of all periods of the Roman Empire are reflections of court fashion, and thus a distant glimpse of the moral climate and social composition of the court.

78
IX
72d
72e
72f

On various occasions, attempts were made to curb excessive expenditure on dress and, more rarely, to impose a form of dress which not only indicated moral restraint, but also suggested a certain social class and shared identity. One of the most influential moves in this direction was made by Augustus, a ruler remarkable for his capacity to reinvent a long-disused tradition and make it appear to have survived unbroken from the distant past. Augustus revived ancient Roman customs in dress with

73 *Detail of a marble portrait bust of a woman, about* AD 210–230, *whose natural hair is clearly shown beneath her wig. At the back of her head the hair is rolled into a flat plait (see fig. 72f).*

such authority that the memory of the revival, if not the tradition itself, survived into late antiquity. The toga for men and, less certainly, the stola for women had republican origins but reached their definitive forms under Augustus. As men played a far greater part than women in political and ceremonial life, and thus attended many more occasions at which more formal dress was required, the toga survived, more or less as Augustus had intended it, for a very long time, though it may be the case that some late Roman *togati* raided ancestral wardrobes for special occasions. Women, on the other hand, appear to have given up wearing the stola (a tubular wool garment joined by straps at the shoulder) by about the time of Trajan. However, women described as *feminae* or *matronae stolatae* (women or matrons entitled to wear the stola) appear in late Roman inscriptions, and a personification of (significantly) Roma wearing the stola was painted on the wall of the Constantinian basilica of St Peter. Evidently the term stola survived, both as an indication of high social rank and in association with the identity of Rome itself, and the form of the stola was well understood in late antiquity. This last point is also clear from the descriptions of the garment given by late Roman lexicographers and commentators.

All peoples wear an overgarment of some kind: in its most basic form, this is a rectangular draped mantle with no fastening. The Greeks wore such a mantle (*himation*); for travelling and manual labour they wore the *chlamys*, a semicircular cloak fastened with a brooch. The Greek mantle was also very popular in Rome, where it was known by the Latin term *pallium*. There is some confusion in the ancient literary sources over the origin of the toga (in Greek *tebenna*). Those authors (Livy, I, 8, and Pliny, *Natural History*, VIII, 48) who claim an Etruscan origin for the *toga praetexta*, a toga worn by children and magistrates which had a band of purple woven as a border along the upper straight edge, are supported by the surviving archaeological evidence, which suggests that, as early as the archaic period, the Etruscans favoured a cloak with a curved hem. Evidently, too, the Etruscans and the Romans liked their clothes to follow the shape of the body, and thus preferred curved garments. The Romans also wore more clothing than the Greeks, mostly favouring a tunic under the heavy *tebenna*. The toga, then, was a mantle with a more or less straight upper edge (though even the corners of this became rounded in the Augustan version) and a curved lower edge.

Originally, according to Aulus Gellius (*Noctes Atticae*, VII, 112), the toga was worn by men and women with no tunic beneath it. Archaeological evidence suggests that the wearing of the *tebenna* by both sexes happened very early, in the sixth century BC. Augustus forbade women to wear the toga, though children of both sexes continued to do so into late antiquity. The republican Roman form of the toga was the so-called *toga exigua* or short toga. The finest surviving example offers a useful link with Etruria in that the subject of the portrait has his name inscribed in Etruscan on the hem. This is the bronze statue of Aulus Metellus, often 74 known as the 'Arringatore' (the Italian word for orator) from his gesture of public address. His toga is short and wrapped close to the body, with a broad band of cloth (*balteus*) passing across the chest from beneath the right elbow. Current opinion places this statue about 100 BC. A funerary relief of about 80 BC from Rome, now in the British Museum, shows a freedman draped in a *toga exigua* as a sign of his newly acquired Roman identity. There are a number of surviving late republican portraits which 75 show a developed version, apparently made of finer cloth, with a wider *balteus* folded across the chest, later hung over the shoulder to make a 50 sling for the right arm. It is not easy to distinguish the late republican *toga exigua* from the Greek *himation* unless the legs of the subject are visible. If there are folds of cloth (*lacinia*) hanging down close to the ankle, then the garment is a toga; if four corners are visible, the garment must be a *himation*. The 'sling' around the right arm, however, and the move to lighter fabric, were surely influenced by contemporary Greek fashion, which had, of course, been present in Rome for some time, especially for the nobility. It was said of the elder Scipio Africanus that he used to walk in the *gymnasium* (presumably of his villa) in Greek mantle and sandals. The toga required laced boots.

Greek fashion was not favoured by Augustus, who was said to have been infuriated by the sight of men in *himatia* or 'dark cloaks' (perhaps a reference to the cheaper garments worn by the poor) thronging the Forum. The emperor went so far as to insist that togas must be worn by men entering the Forum, or indeed any of the surrounding areas, from which Greek mantles were henceforth banned. The toga thus became known as the *vestis forensis* and long retained an association with city dress. 'The toga is what we like to wear in the Forum', claimed the fourth-century writer Nonius (406, 14). 'We wear it in the city, in the

74 *Bronze statue of Aulus Metellus, shown giving an oration; found near Lake Trasimene in central Italy and made about 100 BC. The speaker's name is inscribed in Etruscan on the hem of his garment, which is the short toga as worn in Republican Rome. The portrait head and cropped hair are also Roman in appearance.*

75 *Marble relief of Aurelius Hermia and Aurelia Philematio, freed slaves of Lucius; from Rome and made about 80 BC. In the relief and the texts the couple are portrayed as devoted spouses. Despite their servile origin, they are shown as free Romans, Aurelius dressed in the short toga as worn by Aulus Metellus (fig. 74).*

agora [market-place]', reported the third-century Greek writer Dio Cassius (*Fragment* 145, 2). But the toga was explicitly much more than the Roman equivalent of the pin-striped suit. Non-Romans and the disgraced were forbidden to wear it, according to the younger Pliny (*Epistles*, IV, 11), and Virgil (*Aeneid*, I, 282) celebrated what his ruler Augustus had himself defined as the *gens togata* (the people who wear the toga), a clear distinction intended here between the toga-clad Romans and those who wore the *pallium*.

The idea of the toga as a Roman garment intended for ceremonial use in peacetime was the pervasive element in Augustus' formulation. The emperor Commodus (AD 180–93) caused shock and dismay when, disregarding custom, he ordered spectators of the games to come without their togas. Clearly it was bad form, even in the second century AD, to appear at the imperial dining couch without a toga. The Libyan future emperor Septimius Severus (AD 193–211) arrived at the emperor's dining table wearing a *pallium*, but was able to save embarrassment by accepting a spare toga from the imperial wardrobe. This incident was later interpreted as one of many portents of the outsider Severus' rise to power (Spartianus, *Severus*, 1).

The first inklings of the importance accorded to the toga in the reign
of Augustus appear on the reliefs of the Ara Pacis (Altar of Augustan
Peace, dedicated at Rome in 9 BC), which show the imperial family and
their circle in ceremonial role. Not everyone wears the same kind of toga,
and it seems that the elegantly draped Augustan version was slow to
catch on. The new status of the toga was celebrated by an increase in its
size, and a hitching up of the drapery so that attention could be focused
upon the upper part of the body and not on the ugly bunches of cloth
between the legs. Augustan togas were distinguished by a fold of cloth
(the *sinus*) sweeping down from the right shoulder and by a tuck at the   46
waist (the *umbo*), achieved by pulling up the end of the cloak which had
previously hung against the leg, and drawing it out across the lower
curve of the *sinus*. The *sinus* could easily be raised over the head, in a
gesture often too narrowly interpreted as referring to the performance of
a religious sacrifice. This gesture had a wider as well as a specific
meaning: it conveyed the idea of that most Augustan adjective *pius*
(dutiful and modest). All Augustan portraits that were intended to
impress a wide public are well draped, even to excess.

There are plenty of literary references suggesting that the Romans
found the toga uncomfortable. By the end of the first century AD, we see
the first appearance of a less cumbersome form of draping the toga, if not
a reduction in size. Gradually the *umbo* disappeared and the *sinus* became
more tightly folded so that by the third century the folds lay in thick
bands across the chest (*contabulatio*). It became customary in portraits   76
with this type of toga to show some of the lower folds draped across the
arm or held in the hand. Despite these changes, the toga was no less of a
burden to wear: specially trained servants (*vestiplici*) set the folds in place
with heated tongs (Tertullian, *De pall*. 5, p. 1100 B). Particularly
amusing is the account given by Macrobius (*Satires* III, 13, 4) of the
dandy Hortensius, who checked himself carefully in the mirror before
going out, arranging the folds of his toga with the utmost care.
Hortensius, we are told, considered it a crime should anyone brush
against him in an alley, disarranging his attire.

In time, the association of the toga with Roman identity became
broadly understood: thus, while the majority of surviving statues of
Augustus show him wearing the toga, there is only one known togate
statue of the second-century AD emperor Hadrian. Most statues and

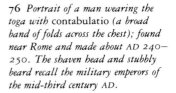

76 *Portrait of a man wearing the toga with* contabulatio *(a broad band of folds across the chest); found near Rome and made about* AD 240–250. *The shaven head and stubbly beard recall the military emperors of the mid-third century* AD.

busts of Hadrian show him in military dress, a fashion much favoured by other second- and third-century emperors. Several surviving statues show him naked, and one statue now in the British Museum, which comes from the sanctuary of Apollo at Cyrene, shows him in Greek dress – surely a reflection of the emperor's personal tastes. By this time it was no longer necessary to advertise the Roman nature of the emperor – everyone who needed to, knew what was Roman and what was not. There was a place in Roman society for those provincials of means who wanted advancement, as most of them did. This is a very different world from that of Augustus, in which most provincials experienced the Romans as oppressive conquerors. From earliest days, though, Rome had distinguished herself as a society open to outsiders, an attitude implying successive redefinitions of personal and group identity.

The stola, meanwhile, had connotations of social rank much more narrowly defined than those of the toga, being reserved for the highest ranking married women in Roman society. It was intended to mark out the Roman matron and define her as untouchable by any but her husband. The garment deliberately emphasised chastity by concealing the body with a wide tube of yellow wool woven in one piece, worn over

the tunic and falling to the ankles. Like the *toga praetexta*, it was decorated with a coloured border, the *instita*. Some stolas, it must be admitted, are reminiscent of pinafores or gymslips of the most unflattering kind, and these are matched by equally constraining hairstyles. Most representations, though, especially those of the Julio-Claudian era, show quite a different garment, reminiscent of modern lingerie and with similar connotations of sexuality. Cut low between the breasts, and suspended from the slimmest of decorative straps, this stola can only be described as suggestive. The majority of these portraits are of the late 30s   72a
or 40s AD, an age hardly known for its moral restraint. It is possible that the fine series of cameo representations of women wearing the stola, all apparently members of the imperial family, were made to commemorate the granting of exceptional honours to these women by the emperor Gaius (Caligula, AD 37–41), honours previously reserved for Augustus' empress Livia and the Vestal Virgins. Some portraits survive of non-imperial women wearing the stola, including one from Pompeii and one   72c
from Velleia in northern Italy. No surviving representations of it appear to be later than the end of the first century AD, though the garment was clearly understood in late antiquity. The fourth-century painting from St Peter's of Roma in a stola is the only full-length representation of the garment to conform to the literary evidence for the appearance of the skirt. It is possible that first-century sculptors, accustomed to bust-length portrayals of women wearing the stola, were ignorant of how the skirt was treated.

The social history of the stola, like that of its female wearers, is harder to recapture than that of the toga, since women were less visible in public life. Nonetheless, it seems likely that the stola underwent a similar process to that of the Augustan toga. It simply ceased to have the definitive and restricted role intended by Augustus when citizenship and the consequent attainment of rank and privilege for very wealthy provincials changed the social composition of the imperial court and the Roman Senate. Indeed, the emperor Hadrian's taste for Greek culture was to deal a body-blow to the Roman identity as conceived by Augustus. More and more Romans were shown bearded, in Greek dress, and were portrayed on their memorial coffins as 'men of culture'.

Jewellery, other than the protective amulet (*bulla*) worn by the children of Roman citizens, or rings used as seals and signs of office, was considered a foreign luxury as unbecoming to the Roman as the dark cloaks banned by Augustus from the Forum at Rome. The elder Pliny records, disapprovingly (*Natural History*, IX, 57):

> I saw Lollia Paulina, who became the first wife of Gaius [Caligula], not at
> a serious or solemn ceremony but at a modest matrimonial banquet,
> covered with interlaced emeralds and pearls, shining all over her head,
> hair, ears, neck and fingers, the total value amounting to 40,000,000
> sesterces . . . nor were they presents from an extravagant emperor, but
> ancestral possessions actually acquired as loot from the provinces.

It may be that this notion, like the emperor's views on ostentatious Hellenistic Greek dress, was derived from the customs of classical Greece, where finds of jewellery in private contexts on sites in the heartlands of central and southern Greece are rare, though no written evidence survives of any proscription on the wearing of jewellery. Nonetheless, like Hellenistic Greek dress, jewellery was much worn in imperial Rome, and appears in a range of surviving Roman portraits, notably in the eastern Mediterranean provinces which produced distinctive regional types of funerary portrait. Among these the most striking are the limestone funerary reliefs of Palmyra, in which women appear to be weighted with gold in the manner of modern bedouin; no less distinctive are the painted mummy portraits and gilded mummy masks of Roman Egypt and some marble sculptures, notably from Cyrenaica (eastern Libya), which have pierced ears, indicating that earrings (and doubtless other jewels that have left no trace) were added in metal.

The multiple jewels worn by the subjects of mummy masks are a striking sign of Roman influence in a very Egyptian form of portrait. On the painted mummy portraits, jewellery often provides a valuable indication of date, showing – together with the hairstyles that mimic those of the imperial court at Rome – that the subjects of these portraits (many of whom were of Greek origin but resident in Egypt) kept up with contemporary fashions in Italy. In that sense, certain types of jewellery are a sign of Roman identity akin to togas and stolas, though many jewels survive that are typical of a certain region of the Roman Empire, such as the enamelled bronze pins popular in the north-west provinces.

Aside from the range of traditional Roman or Greek dress, there existed in antiquity portraits of individuals wearing no clothes at all.

Just as certain clothes denoted a particular social class or occupation, so nudity carried a number of connotations directly related to the context of the portrait. In classical Greek art, male nudity was entirely acceptable for young men in the context of an athletic contest or symposium. Some men, mostly young, appear naked on painted mummy portraits from Roman Egypt; it is likely that these, too, had completed a classical Greek education (*paideia*) in which traditional athletic competition had a place. By contrast, female nudity in Greek art implied the courtesan.

Hellenistic rulers were often portrayed naked, a device effectively distancing them from ordinary mortals and giving them almost divine status. The emperor Augustus was portrayed semi-naked on objects of limited circulation, but in the more overtly imperial climate of later reigns it became acceptable once more to portray the emperor naked on statues that would be seen by many of his subjects.

In the later first century AD there appeared a series of funerary portraits representing ordinary Romans half-draped or unclothed with the deliberate intention of commemorating them as if they were gods. Many such portraits were of freedmen and freedwomen of non-Roman origin, who had gained considerable economic success in the course of the first century AD. No contemporary comments on these portraits survive, though it is likely that they were despised by the established Roman aristocracy, whose portraits remained well covered!

77

39

VII

78

78 *Marble portrait of a woman as victorious Venus, one of a sries of reliefs from her tomb in Rome. The woman's hairstyle is of the early second century* AD, *and she is clothed only across the thighs. She carries a palm branch symbolising victory and is admired by a dove at her feet.*

CHAPTER 10

Epilogue

I t is sometimes claimed that appreciation of the art of portraiture is in decline, a claim belied by the rising number of visitors recorded at the National Portrait Gallery in London in 1994. It may be that the visitors were curious to see the recently opened display of twentieth-century portraits, in which they could find images of recent and contemporary public figures, already well known to viewers of television and readers of newspapers. Portraits of famous figures of earlier times do not always command such attention: we may recall the Roman practice, despised by some commentators, of reusing the torsos of portrait statues of individuals no longer of public interest and fitting them with newly carved portrait heads. If some giants of culture remain ever popular, such as Homer, or, more recently, Shakespeare, others – notably politicians and rulers – are more vulnerable to history and fashion.

In modern times painting, especially in oils, and photography have emerged as media of major importance to portraiture. Sculptured portraits are still made, especially in bronze, but are generally not widely appreciated.

Portraits of the former British prime minister Margaret Thatcher offer much of relevance to the study of portraiture in remote antiquity. Her advisers were highly successful in creating an image that left as strong an impression as her forceful character. Her clothes for formal sittings were invariably severe, suggesting her suitability for a traditionally male role. They were, however, often relieved by a string or two of pearls and a blouse with a flowing bow-tie, a device both expressive of femininity and giving movement to the figure, thereby suggesting energy in greater quantity than that possessed by the men flanking her in suits. The pearls and flowing bow drew the viewer's attention to the neck, and thence to the face, where the eyes, as in Roman portraits, proved the strongest feature. The concentration of movement at the head and neck is also

79 *The Conservative Party Conference, 1981, painted by Paul Brason. Mrs Thatcher addresses the delegates, the message on the wall embodied in her pose, her energy emphasised by the flowing bow-tie. To the right, her husband Denis shields his brow, as if dazed by his wife's authority.*

characteristic of ancient portraiture, and recalls the Roman fashion for portrait busts.

Certain types of formal portrait have survived in forms little changed over the centuries. Principal among these are the images of the British monarch that appear on coinage and in (usually full-length) portraits set up in embassies and other institutions, especially overseas, where Britain is presented to a non-British audience as a monarchy. There has, however, been a reversal of usage of informal portraits. Whereas in antiquity portraits showing members of the imperial family in god-like poses were restricted in circulation to a limited group of individuals whose loyalty was unquestioned, today a similar group of persons might expect to receive a signed informal photograph. Wide circulation of informal royal portraits may be seen as undermining royal status, but many Roman emperors chose to present themselves to their subjects as no more than first citizen, a role that encouraged personal loyalty and fostered an illusion of accessibility. Indeed, the shifting roles of ruler portraiture even today illustrate a maxim that holds true for portraits of any age: however successfully the artist draws out an individual's appearance or character, a portrait always carries more messages than a mere documentary record.

80

80 *Fifty-pence piece, 1969, with bust of Queen Elizabeth II draped in the style of a Roman portrait of the later second century AD (compare pl. IX).*

Further Reading

Breckenridge, J. D., 'The origins of Roman republican portraiture', in H. Temporini (ed.), *Aufstieg und Niedergang der römischen Welt*, I, 4 (Berlin and New York 1973), 826–54

Brilliant, R., *Portraiture* (London 1991)

Richter, G. M. A., *The Portraits of the Greeks*, abridged and revised by R. R. R. Smith (London 1983)

Sebasta, J. L., and L. Bonfante (eds), *The World of Roman Costume* (Wisconsin 1994)

Smith, R. R. R., *Hellenistic Royal Portraits* (Oxford 1988)

Zanker, P., *The Power of Images in the Age of Augustus*, trans. A. Shapiro (Ann Arbor 1988)

Illustration Credits

Index

Numbers in italics refer to figure or plate nos.

Ada 95; *34*
Aeschines 10; *4*
Agrippina the Elder *72a*
Alcibiades 46–7, 83; *IV*
Alexander the Great 11–12, 17, 46, 52–4, 56–7, 59, 65, 83–5; *5–6, 35–6*
Alexandria 53, 60; *2*
Altar of Augustan Peace 71, 102; *49*
Ancestral portraits 12, 55–6, 76–9, 81, 85, 96; *56a–b*
Antiochus I of Syria 56
Antisthenes 43–4; *26*
Antoninus Pius 14, 16, 93, 98; *12, 66*
Aphrodisias 26, 46, 49, 53; *16*
Arbinnas of Xanthus *33*
Aristogeiton 35–6; *23*
Aristotle 41, 46, 54; *29*
Artemisia 52, 95; *V*
Athens 7–8, 12, 15, 32, 36–7, 39, 41, 43, 60, 88, 91
Athletic victories 28–9, 31–2, 40; *18–19, 21, 25*
Augustus 18, 44, 46, 56, 61–71, 73–4, 80–1, 85, 93, 97–8, 100–4, 106; *44–8, VI, VII*
Aulus Metellus 100; *74*

Beard 14, 39, 54, 64, 83–93, 104; *33, 37, 43a, 61, 65–8, 76–7, 1*
Bryaxis 52
Bust, portrait 41, 82, 90, 104, 109; *16, 39, 42, 48, 53, 54a, 57–8, 61, 63, 65–7, 71–2, 76, 80*

Cameo portraits 25, 58, 68, 85, 87, 104; *72*
Carthage 12, 25; *7, II*
Chares of Teichioussa 28, 50; *17*
Cheilon 28–9
Children, portraits of 22, 25, 71; *47, 49, 64*
Cicero 41, 86

Cleopatra VII of Egypt 65–6, 74, 96; *52*
Coinage, portraits on 10, 13, 25, 50–1, 54, 56–8, 64, 68–70, 79–80, 86–7, 92, 109; *8a–b 31, 35–6, 43, 45a, 47, 56, 68, 80*
Collectors, Roman 8, 41–6
Cologne 29
Commodus 14, 101
Constantine 15, 59, 93
Corinth 7, 47, 84, 87
Court portraiture, copying of 73–5, 81–2, 90, 94, 97–8, 105; *37, 50–3*
Cyprus 58; *37*
Cyrenaica 58, 82, 105; *58*
Cyrene 31, 50, 103; *40, 66–7, III, IX*

Damnatio memoriae 61–2
Darius 53, 56; *5*
Death-masks 76–8, 105; *54*
Delphi 7, 29, 52, 55; *19*
Demetrios of Alopeke 39, 40
Demosthenes 10, 46; *3*
Diadem 59, 68, 74, 79; *39–40, 52*
Diocletian 14–15
Discobolus 28; *18*
Domitian 14, 62, 87
Doryphoros (spear-carrier) 39, 45
Dress 13, 15, 18, 25–6, 54, 56, 69, 72–3, 94–108; *1, 9, 19, 22, 33, 42, 44, 46, 55, 65–6, 69–72, 74–6, 78–80, cover, VIII, XII*

Egypt 24, 31, 53–5, 57, 60, 62, 65, 70, 74, 82, 88, 105–6; *38–9, 42, 77, VII, VIII*
Eikon 16, 55
Ephesus (Library of Celsus at) 52
Epicurus 41, 43–4; *26*
Etruscan dress 83, 99–100
Euphronios 34; *22*
Euripides 8

Faustina the Elder 16, 24; *12*
Flamininus, Titus Quinctius 86–7

Freedmen, portraits of 21, 72–5, 80–1, 100, 106; *50, 53, 57, 75, 78*
Funerary portraits 13, 17–18, 21–2, 24–5, 29, 32, 39, 72ff, 82, 84, 90, 92, 100, 104–5; *9–11, 15, 50, 53–5, 57–8, 62, 71, 75, 77–8*

Gaius Caesar 69–70; *47*
Gaius (Caligula) 104–5
Gallienus 14; *8b*
Geneleos group 32; *20*
Germanicus Caesar 62–3, 81; *42, 49*
Glykilla *10*
Group portraits 7, 21, 31, 35, 47, 55, 58, 69–71, 80; *10–12, 20, 23, 26, 29, 34, 49, 50, 53, 57, 62, 75, 79, V*

Hadrian 14, 85–6, 88, 90–2, 98, 102–4; *8, 12, 23, 65, IX*
Hairstyles 13, 54, 73–4, 94–5, 97–8, 105; *6, 27, 44, 54, 58, 60–1, 64, 70–3, II, III, IX*
Harmodios 35–6; *23*
Hellenistic kingdoms 10–12, 39, 45, 84, 96; *32*
Hellenistic ruler-portraits 11–12, 44, 46, 50–60, 65–6, 74, 83, 97, 106; *5, 35–6, 38–40, 43b, 44, 70*
Herculaneum 44, 97; *27*
Herm, portrait 37, 41; *1, 3–4, 14, 24, 27*
Herodes Atticus 21–3, 52, 84; *12, 59*
Hesiod *frontispiece, 30*
Hipparchus 35; *23*
Homer 23–4, 34, 45, 88, 108; *13–14, 30*

Idreus 52; *34*
Inscribed portraits 18, 25, 28, 50, 53, 57–8, 72, 80; *15–17, 27*

Jewellery 13, 104–5, 108; *10*, *VIII*
Julius Caesar 13, 61, 64–6, 79–80, 86; *56c*

'Kaloskagathos' 34, 39; *22*
Kharei of Xanthus *31*

Laurel wreath 59, 68; *37*
Leagros 34, 36
Leochares 52
Licinii, Tomb of the 6
Livia 70, 73, 86, 104; *51*
Lucius Caesar 69–70; *47*
Lucius Verus 84; *12*
Lycia 10, 50; *32–3*
Lysippos 39, 42

Macedon 10, 11, 52, 54, 57, 84, 86; *3–4*, *32*
Macrinus 93; *68*
Mainz 68; *VII*
Mantle (*himation*; *pallium*) 99–101
Marcus Aurelius 84, 93; *12*, *67*, *68*
Mark Antony 64–6; *41*
Marriage portraits 17–18, 21–2; *75*
Mausoleum at Halicarnassus 21, 23, 51–2, 95; *11*, *70*, *V*
Mausolus of Caria 10–11, 21–2, 51–2, 95; *11*, *34*, *V*
Maximinus Thrax *8a*
Meroe 62–3, 68; *VII*
Military portraits 12, 14, 28, 39, 40, 53–4, 59, 62, 68–9, 79, 85; *1*, *5*, *7*, *9*, *42*, *55*, *60*, *65*, *66*
Mithradates VI of Pontus 36
Moneyers, ancestral portraits on coins of 79; *56a & b*
Mosaics, portraits in 15; *5*, *29*
Mummy masks 105
Mutilated portraits 44, 62; *42*, *VII*
Myron 28; *18*

Nero 13–14, 87; *8*
Nudity 54, 69, 75, 103, 105–7; *39*, *55*, *63*, *77–8*

Octavian (later Augustus) 13, 64–6, 69–70, 80, 85–6; *43–4*, *46*
Olbia 46, 88

Olympia 7, 21, 23, 29, 37, 52, 55; *12*
Orators, portraits of 25–6, 32, 50, 84, 100; *3–5*, *15*, *74*, *79*, *cover*
Ostia 37, 47; *28*

Painted portraits 24, 82, 105–6, 108; *77*, *VIII*
Palmyrene portraits 105
Panyassis of Halicarnassus 45; *27*
Pausanias, king of Sparta 26; *16*
Pergamum 54–5, 66
Pericles 8, 39, 42, 91; *1*, *65*
Persian empire 7, 11, 51–3; *32–3*
Persian wars 8, 35
Pheidias 39, 45
Philip V of Macedon 86
Philosophers, portraits of 8, 42–4, 46–7, 49, 84, 92–3; *2*, *26*, *67*
Philosophical Schools 15, 44, 46, 49; *16*
Photographic portraits 18, 25, 108–9
Pindar 26, 46; *16*
'Pioneers' (vase-painters) 34; *22*
Plato 8, 41; *29*
Poets, portraits of 8, 45–6, 84; *frontispiece*, *16*, *30*, *1*
Polykleitos 39, 45, 66; *25*
Polyzales of Gela 31; *19*
Pompeii 45, 53, 104; *5*
Pompey 12, 85; *6*, *7*
Priene 95; *70*
Proclus 25–6; *15*
'Pseudo-Seneca' *frontispiece*, *30*
Ptolemies of Egypt 53–60, 74; *35*, *38–40*
Pythagoras 45–6

'Rampin' rider 32–3; *21*
Retrospective portraits 23–4; *frontispiece*, *7*, *13–14*, *16*, *24*, *26–9*
Reused portraits 62, 108
Rhodes *41*
Rings, portraits on 58, 60; *72a–f*
Roman Empire 12–13, 41, 45, 48, 55–6, 59, 71, 78–9, 85–8, 90, 94, 98, 103
Roman Forum, 81, 100
Roman Republic 11–14, 41, 44, 46, 57, 66, 70–1, 74–82, 96
Roman ruler-portraits 11–13, 46,

55–6, 60, 66, 68, 70, 97, 109; *7*, *8*, *42–9*, *51*, *56c*, *63*, *65–8*, *72a*
Rome 12–13, 41, 43, 47, 60–1, 66, 71–2, 74–5, 77, 80–1, 83, 86, 96, 99, 102; *46*, *49–50*, *53*, *56–7*, *75*, *76*
Rosetta stone 55

Sabina *12*, *72d*, *IX*
Samos 32, 46; *20*
Sanctuaries, portraits displayed in 7, 21, 31, 55–6, 80, 92, 95, 103; *17*, *20–1*, *34*, *37*, *70*
Sarcophagi, portraits on 25; *15*
Scipio Africanus (the Elder) 100
Seals, portraits on 57–8; *60*
Seated figures 18; *10*, *17*, *20*, *28*, *33*, *69*, *79*
Septimius Severus 14, 101
Sicily 83; *19*
Skopas 52
Smikros 34
Smyrna 62, *64*
Socrates 8, 42–3, 46; *2*, *29*
Sophocles 8; *29*, *1*
Sparta 7–8, 12, 26, 47, 88; *28*, *IV*
Stola 99, 103–5; *72a & c*
Syria 54–5, 57

Tegea 52; *34*
Thatcher, Margaret, portraits of 108–9; *79*
Themistocles 36–7, 39; *24*
Tiberius 68–70; *48*, *VII*
Timotheos 52
Toga 68, 71, 76, 79, 96, 99–100, 102, 104–5; *46*, *VII*
Trajan 14, 86, 92, 98–9; *63*

Veiled portraits 68; *44*, *46*
Verism 78, 85, 96; *41*, *55*
Vespasian 13, 82; *7*
Vessels, portraits on 34, 58; *22*, *38*, *69*

Welschbillig 46
Wigs 98; *73*
Women, portraits of 22–3, 95; *10–12*, *20*, *34*, *38*, *50–2*, *57–8*, *62*, *69–73*, *75*, *78–80*

Xanthus 50